" ".... Can this cockpit hold
The vasty fields of France? or may we cram
Within this wooden O the very casques
That did affright the air at Agincourt?"
W. Sh.

This book is no cockpit, but,
the bumper harvest of drawings
from pen-active days, has, despite omissions, certainly
crammed some of the pages. However,
the interested reader can be relied upon
to accept this, & to pore over the tiny details.
For does not E.F. Schumacher say;-
"Small is beautiful." 1911-1977

Cased, limited edition, signed & numbered;-
0 947620 02 8
Soft back edition;- 0 947620 03 6

TRAVELS

IN
SCOTLAND,
ENGLAND,
& OVERSEAS, TO

EUROPE
NEW YORK
CANADA
NEW ZEALAND
W. AUSTRALIA
THAILAND.

❖ ❖ ❖

These records are my
'SPOILS OF TIME'
FROM NEAR & FAR
in an assembly of separate
self contained pages about jaunts which have
stimulated the eager eye, alerted the senses,
& given the author a wider world both
for recall & contemplation.

"All the mighty world of eye and ear" W.W

For
all my friends
at home here
and abroad,

this collection of pages,
[5 books in one]

hoping they will find
congenial echoes
here & there;

and for all those
whose sense of wonder
never fails to illuminate
the commonplace.

"I was for that time lifted above earth
And possessed joys not promised at my birth."
W. WORDSWORTH

☆　　☆　　☆　　☆　　☆

"Your book is not like a novel with page after page to turn
in rapid succession" said H.J.C. "I open your book when
relaxed in bed & study one page or perhaps 2, each night." !

"Like many elderlies" said F.D.G. "I have sleepless periods
during the night. For an interval, I open, not a novel, but your
book, & select one page to read & contemplate. Just the answer!"

"A 'dipping into' book" said E·W·B· "which one savours
deliciously in small mouthfuls."

"I keep your book on the coffee table," said Jean M
& do a page over a cup."
Just exactly what I do," ejaculated Effie R

"I keep one set of your books in the visitors' room," remarked Pamela R.

"The quotations dotted about give me much pleasure" enthused Susan G.

CONTENTS

" Oh joy! that in our embers
Is something that doth live,
That nature yet remembers
What was so fugitive !
The thoughts of our past years in me doth breed
Perpetual benediction. "
w.w.

2

"Yet longing comes upon him to fare forth." E. POUND

INTERCITY TRAINS.

One of the best moments for me is when I sink serenely into my booked seat.
The relief! You drop the reins, belong neither here nor there, become
for an interval a self indulgent non entity, a mere passenger.

Dive into a book? write? crossword? draw? knit? patience?
No, not yet. Just ruminate. Let the wheel music wash over you.
Listen to the rhythmic train talk:-

| whirr & purr | groan & moan | rumble & mumble | roar & shout | as it races & chases |
| slide & glide, | croon & drone, | shudder & shake, | whistle & shriek, | hurries & scurries, |

scorching & zooming its way along the straight [or curved] track.

And the folk aboard? An orchestration of human voices,
tenor, bass, childish treble? a babel of tongues, guttural sonorous?
hoarse, nasal, strident? giggles & laughter, gabble & chatter,
dialect, brogue, vernacular? or is there human silence?

NO CRYING BABIES TODAY. JUST JOLLY LAUGHING ONES.

How children & toddlers love that long wobbling passage way!
How the twosomes & foursomes relish a bout of chess & a hand of whist.
How the bookworms seize this leisure for guiltless escapes.
How the crossword addicts cudgel their brains.
How commuters rely on it for sedulous brief-case work.
How the loners revel in a private world of head phone diversion.
How the retirees enjoy the folk, a chat, the movie on either side, & a nodding doze!

FOLK WHO DON'T USE INTERCITY TRAINS MISS A VERY GOOD SLICE OF LIFE!

Now what a hustle & bustle as the train slows down & glides to a halt.
Bundles, bags & baggage, hauled & handled, disappears. New faces aboard
now, They settle down, & off we go. What scenes to L. & R as we gather
speed, eating the miles. Oh! there's a face must be drawn. But
it moves of course, & the train rocks. NOT SO EASY!

There's the Sutton Bank White Horse, & here's Durham Cathedral
spectacular, high above the city; now the castle peak of Lindisfarne out to sea,
& these are the 3 Berwick-on-Tweed bridges. The sugar loaf of Bass Rock
just shows, & now the rock of Arthur's Seat towers ahead. Let's alight at
Waverley, & stretch our legs on its craggy slopes above Edinburgh.

INTERCITY TRAINS ACROSS EUROPE, IN BELGIUM, NETHERLANDS, FRANCE, ITALY, GREECE, NORWAY, SWEDEN; ALSO
WHITE RUSSIA, UZBEKISTAN, NEW SOUTH WALES, & THE BLISSFUL CANADIAN PACIFIC RLY,
have each given tremendous interest & pleasure to me.

LOOKING AT SCOTLAND

27 brimful pages,
separately entitled,
on various aspects of Scotland,
noted & sketched
during many travels.

✢   ✢   ✢   ✢   ✢

and references to much else including:-

ABERDEEN, DUNDEE, ELGIN, HADDINGTON, INVERNESS,
KIRKCALDY, OBAN, PERTH, ST.ANDREWS, STIRLING, & SO ON,

in this diverse country where no town is
farther than 60 miles from the sea,
where the islands number 787,
& the coastline measures 2,900 m/s? approx

See further pages about Scotland in
books listed on back cover.

"Mountains that like giants stand
To sentinel the enchanted land"
SIR WALTER SCOTT   LADY OF THE LAKE.

"In the highlands,
in the country places,
Where the old plain men
have rosy faces,
And the young fair maidens
Quiet eyes." R.L.S.

"Here, rivers in the sea were lost
There mountains to the skies were toss't
Here tumbling billows marked the coast
With surging foam ---
There, distant shone Arts' lofty boast
The lovely dome." R.Burns.

Dr Samuel Johnson 1709-1784
& James Boswell back in 1773
made their Scotland Tour to the Hebrides.

If ever there was an intrepid tour for a metropolitan
to undertake, surely this was it. Roads of a sort petered
out after Inverness, then their travelling was of the roughest:
horseback, shanks pony on rocky tracks, or boat, in the fickle
W. Highland weather, unpredictable, sometimes fine, often unfavourable.
'A STOUT HEART TAE A STEY BRAE' was req.ᵈ, a dogged persistence, a strong
constitution, & a compulsive interest, & these they each undoubtedly had.

My astonishment at their achievement was at its height in Coll 1977
whither ʷᵉ sailed in comfort, & at Braechacha Castle whither ʷᵉ cycled easily.

James Boswell on
Dr Samuel Johnson :-

'He read tonight to himself
a great deal of my journal, &
said "This will be a great
treasure to us some years hence."

Dr J :- "I cannot but laugh
to think of myself roving
among the Hebrides at
sixty. I wonder where I
shall rove at four score?"

'Breacacha [Spotted Field]
is enamelled in summer
with clover & daisies,
young Col told me.'

WHAT WEATHER THEY SOMETIMES HAD :-
'The weather was worse than
yesterday. I felt imprisoned!'

'During the day our bedchambers
were common to all the house.
Servants eat in Dr J's & mine was
a general rendezvous for all —'

'Our sails were very bad & in
danger of being torn to pieces.
Sparks of burning peat flew so
much about I dreaded the vessel
might take fire. We often lay so
much on one side I trembled
lest we should be overset
in this prodigious sea.'

O. Goldsmith
on Dr Johnson :-

"If his pistol misses fire,
he knocks you down
with the buttend of it."

J.B.: "Dr J appears to me like
a great mill into which
a subject is thrown
to be ground."

'Whisky was served in a
shell according to the
ancient Highland custom.
Dr J would not partake of
it, but drank some water
out of the shell.'

"That man is little to be envied whose patriotism would not gain force upon the
plains of Marathon, or whose piety would not grow warmer among the ruins of Iona." Dr J.

Of all the waterfalls I know in Scotland, of cataracts & cascades, of overspills & splashes, from the highest to the humblest, from torrent to trickle, roaring fortissimo or tinkling treble, the remote FALLS OF GLOMACH will ever haunt me.

A MEMORY & IMAGINATIVE MIX

Difficult of access did you say? That was challenge enough to set M·M·B's feet tingling impatiently. Any mountain walk or exploration was, for her, preferable to city sights.

So, CAR LESS, [in 1947 & 48] & using cycles & legs, we set off indomitably & achieved the Falls by the hard ways on 3 diverse occasions, not without considerable misgivings on my part & near heart failure on occasions.

WATCH YOUR STEP! OUR ROUTES WERE:-

Cycle from our cottage near Balmacara along L.Alsh & L.Duich for Dorusduain, & park bikes. Climb the hillside & contour, then make for the Bealach na Stroine [Pass of the Nose] & so on to the head of the gorge. TAKE A COMPASS

OR

Climb up & thro' Bealach an Sgairne [Rumbling Pass] & by Loch Bhealaich, across boggy moorland & by smaller lochs which feed the Glomach to head of gorge. TAKE A COMPASS

OR

Cycle by L.Long & Glen Elchaig, cross slippery stepping stones of burn in spate, & climb the treacherous steeps to the Falls.

✤　✤　✤　✤　✤

TODAY, BRIDGE, STEPS, TRACKS, SAFETY BARRIERS, MAKE THE SIGHT EASILY REACHED BY TOURISTS.

I THOUGHT OF COLERIDGE'S KUBLA KHAN:-
"But oh! that deep romantic chasm which slanted Down the green hill athwart a cedarn cover! A savage place!...?

'And from this chasm with ceaseless turmoil seething A mighty fountain momently was forced.' S.T.C.

Glomach means wild, savage, forbidding, a meaning made only too clear to us as we pursued our goal.

FROM THE BOGS & LOCHS OF THE HIGH GLEN THE WATER GATHERS TO PLUNGE OVER THE PRECIPICE 300' DOWN ITS RAVINE & AGAIN ANOTHER 50' INTO THE CHASM BELOW. PARTS ARE CRYPTICALLY HIDDEN AWAY BY PROJECTING ROCK, SO A TOTAL VIEW IS IMPOSSIBLE. WHEN IN HURTLING SPATE, WHAT A CRYSTAL DANCE OF SPRAY, WHAT A DEAFENING ROAR!

THE FIVE SISTERS OF KINTAIL ABOVE GLEN SHIEL

The sight of these snowy Sisters pricking thro' mist to blue skies, graces all the hilltop views hereabout in Kintail. WE MUST SET FOOT ON TOP.

M·M·B's compulsive urge to climb, & her shrewd weather sense took us up. In spite of our weight of years, she struggled on wise & undaunted & I followed. So in propitious circumstances we achieved the high panoramic ridges & the Saddle, on either side of this awe inspiring Glen of Shiel.

DR JOHNSON HEROICALLY TRAVELLED THIS WILD, MAGNIFICENTLY SCENIC GLEN IN 1773

"From scenes like these old Scotia's grandeur springs That makes her loved at home revered abroad."
wrote Robert Burns.

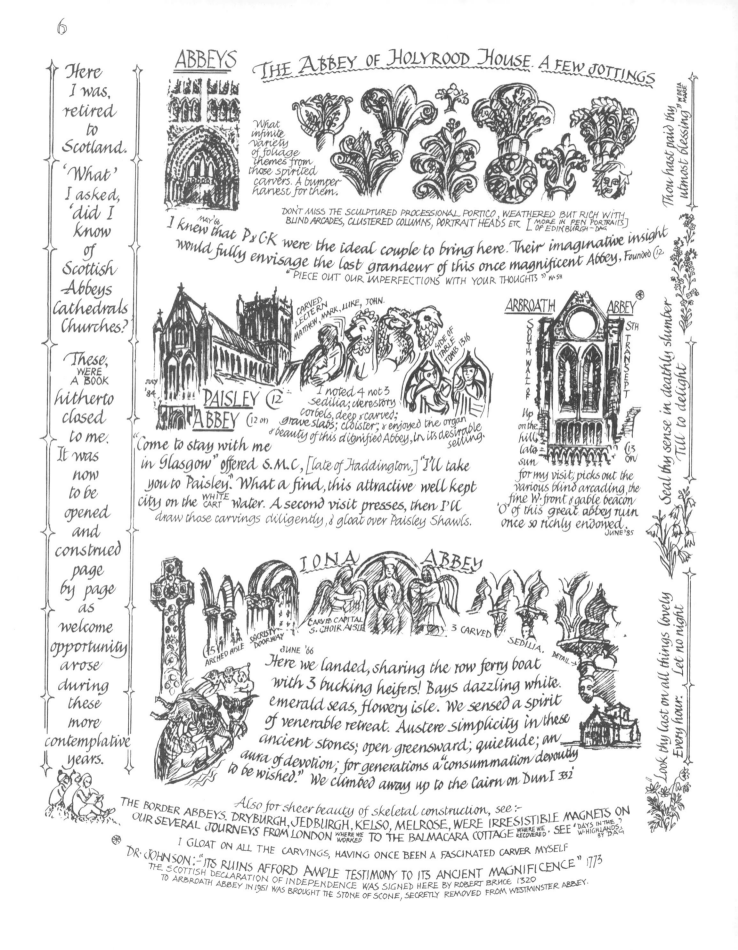

Here I was, retired to Scotland. 'What' I asked, 'did I know of Scottish Abbeys Cathedrals Churches?

These, WERE A BOOK hitherto closed to me. It was now to be opened and construed page by page as welcome opportunity arose during these more contemplative years.

ABBEYS

THE ABBEY OF HOLYROOD HOUSE. A FEW JOTTINGS

What infinite variety of foliage themes from those spirited carvers. A bumper harvest for them.

DON'T MISS THE SCULPTURED PROCESSIONAL PORTICO, WEATHERED BUT RICH WITH BLIND ARCADES, CLUSTERED COLUMNS, PORTRAIT HEADS ETC [MORE IN PEN PORTRAITS OF EDINBURGH — DAG]

MAY '66 I knew that P & CK were the ideal couple to bring here. Their imaginative insight would fully envisage the lost grandeur of this once magnificent Abbey, Founded (12 "PIECE OUT OUR IMPERFECTIONS WITH YOUR THOUGHTS " W. SH

CARVED LECTERN MATTHEW, MARK, LUKE, JOHN.

SIDE OF TABLE TOMB 1316

JULY '84 **PAISLEY** (12 **ABBEY** (12 on

I noted 4 not 3 Sedilia; clerestory corbels, deep & carved; grave slabs; cloister; & enjoyed the organ & beauty of this dignified Abbey, in its desirable setting.

"Come to stay with me in Glasgow" offered S.M.C, [late of Haddington,] "I'll take you to Paisley". What a find, this attractive well kept city on the WHITE CART Water. A second visit presses, then I'll draw those carvings diligently, & gloat over Paisley Shawls.

ARBROATH ABBEY 5TH SOUTH WALL OF TRANSEPT

Up on the hill late sun for my visit, picks out the various blind arcading, the fine W. front & gable beacon 'O' of this great abbey ruin once so richly endowed. JUNE '85 (13 on

I O N A   A B B E Y

CARVED CAPITAL S. CHOIR AISLE 3 CARVED SEDILIA. DETAIL.

15 TH ARCHED AISLE SACRISTY DOORWAY

JUNE '66 Here we landed, sharing the row ferry boat with 3 bucking heifers! Bays dazzling white. emerald seas, flowery isle. We sensed a spirit of venerable retreat. Austere simplicity in these ancient stones; open greensward; quietude; an aura of devotion; for generations a "consummation devoutly to be wished." We climbed away up to the Cairn on Dun I 332

Also for sheer beauty of skeletal construction, see:- THE BORDER ABBEYS. DRYBURGH, JEDBURGH, KELSO, MELROSE, WERE IRRESISTIBLE MAGNETS ON OUR SEVERAL JOURNEYS FROM LONDON WHERE WE WORKED TO THE BALMACARA COTTAGE WHERE WE RECOVERED. SEE 'DAYS IN THE W. HIGHLANDS,' BY DAG

I GLOAT ON ALL THE CARVINGS, HAVING ONCE BEEN A FASCINATED CARVER MYSELF

DR. JOHNSON :- "ITS RUINS AFFORD AMPLE TESTIMONY TO ITS ANCIENT MAGNIFICENCE" 1773 THE SCOTTISH DECLARATION OF INDEPENDENCE WAS SIGNED HERE BY ROBERT BRUCE 1320 TO ARBROATH ABBEY IN 1951 WAS BROUGHT THE STONE OF SCONE, SECRETLY REMOVED FROM WESTMINSTER ABBEY.

Thou hast paid thy utmost blessing" MORIA MARE

Seal thy sense in deathly slumber Till to delight

Look thy last on all things lovely Every hour. Let no night

DUNFERMLINE ABBEY

Geology gave Dunfermline Royal Burgh a glorious hill site for its dominating Norman Abbey on the lip of the glen. History gave great names to this linen weaving town:- Q. Margaret 1045/1093 of course; James I 1394, Charles I 1600 both born here; Robert Bruce 1329 buried here; Scottish Capital for 200yrs, & industrialist Andrew Carnegie b 1835 gave his great beneficence. Views? YES! across the Firth to Pentland Hills Trees? YES! in rich profusion along the glen of Pittencrieff Park.

Here we took a picnic, & the elderly gent on our seat confided :- "I come here every day [or Carnegie's Library if wet] it gives the wife a break." Astrid, from Sweden 1983 rejoined: "So should I if living here. What a philanthropist Carnegie was! All this bounty! All from that humble cottage!" I recalled Crabbe's lines:-

"THIS BOOKS CAN DO, NOR THIS ALONE THEY GIVE NEW VIEWS TO LIFE, AND TEACH US HOW TO LIVE..."

NORMAN NAVE FINELY PROPORTIOND

ANDREW CARNEGIE PITTENCRIEFF PARK.

THE ABBEY CHURCH 1150 MEDIEVAL TOWER & NAVE + MODERN CHURCH BUILT OVER OLD CHOIR FOUNDATIONS. ALSO BENEDICTINE MONASTERY WALLS

DOOCOT IN THE PARK BATTLEMENTED!

CLOCK TOWER CITY CHAMBERS

ROUGH SKETCH STEPPED BUTTRESSES TO GROUND LEVEL. WHY AM I SO FOND OF BUTTRESSES?

FLORAL JOLLIFICATIONS & CURLICUES OF THE GREAT CURVED IRONWORK GATES OF PITTENCRIEFF PARK. PREVIOUS VISITS WITH C.F

Pittencrieff Park was Carnegie's paradise, for him the most sacred spot on earth.

CULROSS

Pure delight is this unique historic little Royal Burgh, once large & prosperous with coalmining, salt panning, ironwork [girdles]; one of Fife's 'fringe of gold' towns "round the beggars mantle" said James VI.

We plunged steeply down the hillside from the Abbey ruins 1217 & trade marked tomb stones; views ahead across the Firth; down Tanner's Brae by Snuff cottage, "WHA WAD HA' THOCHT IT, THAT NOSES WAD HA' BOCHT IT" past Butcher's Hse 1664 to the Mercat Cross.

There the astonishing 'Study', & the 'Nunnery' 1609, the 'Ark', & other dated 1577 pantiled houses, cobbled streets with "crown o' the causey," & so to the Shore's Town House & 'Palace' with its maze of little rooms & terraced garden.

"The shore for our picnic?" "Yes" said Astrid '67 "this spot with a view. I'm sold on this charming village. Much gratitude to the N.T. for their restoration of it."

CLOCK TOWER TOWN HSE ON STONEHAVEN

THE STUDY OUTLOOK TOWER A CURIOUS CROW'S NEST OR IVORY CASTLE

ALABASTER MONUMENT FIGURES G. BRUCE FAMILY 1642 3 SONS 5 DAUGHTERS

LACE EDGED COLLARS & RUFFS & WHAT SLEEVES! ALL FRILLS FLOWERS & FURBELOWS MOST METICULOUSLY CARVED & DIFFERENT FROM EACH OTHER.

3 OF THE 'PALACE' GABLES, [SIR GEORGE BRUCE] BARREL VAULT IN MASTER BEDROOM, PAINTED CEILINGS* MANY HAPPY VISITS HERE

A MOST ENLIGHTENING N.T. CUSTODIAN HELPED US

BACK CAUSEWAY, MID CAUSEWAY, WEE CAUSEWAY, UNITE HERE AT THE CROSS.

* All flesche is grasse, and withereth lyk the haye, And warneth us how weill to live, bot not how long to waye."

"Reading maketh a full man, conference a ready man, writing an exact man" wrote F. Bacon 1561-1626

"Give me, kind heaven, a private station, A mind serene for contemplation." JOHN GAY 1685-1732

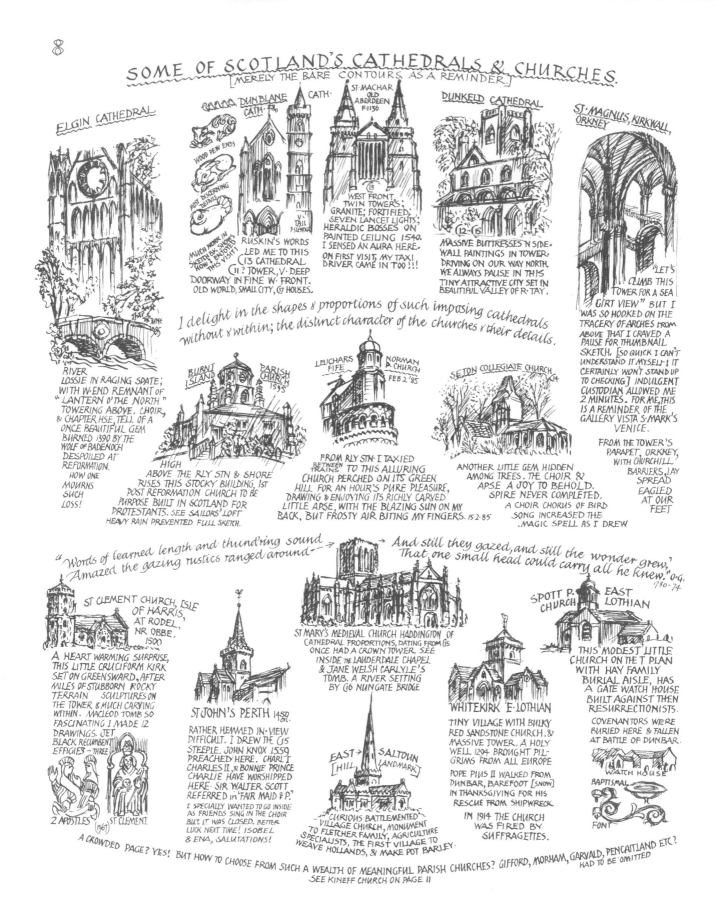

8

SOME OF SCOTLAND'S CATHEDRALS & CHURCHES.
[MERELY THE BARE CONTOURS, AS A REMINDER.]

ELGIN CATHEDRAL

DUNBLANE CATH.

WOOD PEW ENDS

MOST DISCERNING DETAILS

MUCH WORK IN SKETCH BK·SHOWS HOW I ENJOYED THIS VISIT

RUSKIN'S WORDS LED ME TO THIS C13 CATHEDRAL C11? TOWER, V. DEEP DOORWAY IN FINE W. FRONT. OLD WORLD, SMALL CITY, C17 HOUSES.

ST·MACHAR OLD ABERDEEN F·1130 CATH.

WEST FRONT, TWIN TOWERS; GRANITE; FORTIFIED; SEVEN LANCET LIGHTS; HERALDIC BOSSES ON PAINTED CEILING 1540. I SENSED AN AURA HERE. ON FIRST VISIT, MY TAXI DRIVER CAME IN TOO!!!

DUNKELD CATHEDRAL

MASSIVE BUTTRESSES 'N SIDE. WALL PAINTINGS IN TOWER. DRIVING ON OUR WAY NORTH, WE ALWAYS PAUSE IN THIS TINY ATTRACTIVE CITY SET IN BEAUTIFUL VALLEY OF R·TAY.

ST·MAGNUS, KIRKWALL, ORKNEY,

"LET'S CLIMB THIS TOWER FOR A SEA GIRT VIEW" BUT I WAS SO HOOKED ON THE TRACERY OF ARCHES FROM ABOVE THAT I CRAVED A PAUSE FOR THUMBNAIL SKETCH. [SO QUICK I CAN'T UNDERSTAND IT MYSELF· IT CERTAINLY WON'T STAND UP TO CHECKING] INDULGENT CUSTODIAN ALLOWED ME 2 MINUTES. FOR ME, THIS IS A REMINDER OF THE GALLERY VISTA S·MARK'S VENICE.

I delight in the shapes & proportions of such imposing cathedrals without & within; the distinct character of the churches & their details.

RIVER LOSSIE IN RAGING SPATE; WITH W·END REMNANT OF "LANTERN O' THE NORTH" TOWERING ABOVE, CHOIR, & CHAPTER HSE· TELL OF A ONCE BEAUTIFUL GEM BURNED 1390 BY THE WOLF OF BADENOCH DESPOILED AT REFORMATION. HOW ONE MOURNS SUCH LOSS!

BURNT ISLAND PARISH CHURCH 1595

HIGH ABOVE THE RLY STN & SHORE RISES THIS STOCKY BUILDING, 1ST POST REFORMATION CHURCH TO BE PURPOSE BUILT IN SCOTLAND FOR PROTESTANTS. SEE SAILORS' LOFT HEAVY RAIN PREVENTED FULL SKETCH.

LEUCHARS FIFE NORMAN P. CHURCH FEB 2 '85

FROM RLY STN I TAXIED BETWEEN TRAINS TO THIS ALLURING CHURCH PERCHED ON ITS GREEN HILL FOR AN HOUR'S PURE PLEASURE, DRAWING & ENJOYING ITS RICHLY CARVED LITTLE APSE, WITH THE BLAZING SUN ON MY BACK, BUT FROSTY AIR BITING MY FINGERS. 15·2·85

SETON COLLEGIATE CHURCH

ANOTHER LITTLE GEM HIDDEN AMONG TREES. THE CHOIR & APSE A JOY TO BEHOLD. SPIRE NEVER COMPLETED. A CHOIR CHORUS OF BIRD SONG INCREASED THE MAGIC SPELL AS I DREW

FROM THE TOWER'S PARAPET, ORKNEY, WITH CHURCHILL BARRIERS, LAY SPREAD EAGLED AT OUR FEET

"Words of learned length and thund'ring sound Amazed the gazing rustics ranged around→ *→And still they gazed, and still the wonder grew, That one small head could carry all he knew." O·G. 1730-74*

ST CLEMENT CHURCH, ISLE OF HARRIS, AT RODEL, NR OBBE. 1500

A HEART WARMING SURPRISE, THIS LITTLE CRUCIFORM KIRK SET ON GREENSWARD, AFTER MILES OF STUBBORN ROCKY TERRAIN SCULPTURES ON THE TOWER & MUCH CARVING WITHIN. MACLEOD TOMB SO FASCINATING I MADE 12 DRAWINGS. JET BLACK RECUMBENT EFFIGIES – THREE

2 APOSTLES (1967) ST CLEMENT.

ST JOHN'S PERTH 1450 on·

RATHER HEMMED IN·VIEW DIFFICULT. I DREW THE C15 STEEPLE. JOHN KNOX 1559 PREACHED HERE. CHARL I CHARLES II, & BONNIE PRINCE CHARLIE HAVE WORSHIPPED HERE· SIR WALTER SCOTT REFERRED in 'FAIR MAID & P.'
I SPECIALLY WANTED TO GO INSIDE AS FRIENDS SING IN THE CHOIR BUT IT WAS CLOSED. BETTER LUCK NEXT TIME! ISOBEL & ENA, SALUTATIONS!

ST MARY'S MEDIEVAL CHURCH HADDINGTON OF CATHEDRAL PROPORTIONS, DATING FROM C15 ONCE HAD A CROWN TOWER. SEE INSIDE the LAUDERDALE CHAPEL & JANE WELSH CARLYLE'S TOMB. A RIVER SETTING BY C16 NUNGATE BRIDGE

EAST→ SALTOUN [HILL LANDMARK]

CURIOUS BATTLEMENTED VILLAGE CHURCH, MONUMENT TO FLETCHER FAMILY, AGRICULTURE SPECIALISTS. THE FIRST VILLAGE TO WEAVE HOLLANDS, & MAKE POT BARLEY.

WHITEKIRK E·LOTHIAN

TINY VILLAGE WITH BULKY RED SANDSTONE CHURCH· & MASSIVE TOWER. A HOLY WELL 1294 BROUGHT PILGRIMS FROM ALL EUROPE POPE PIUS II WALKED FROM DUNBAR, BAREFOOT [SNOW] IN THANKSGIVING FOR HIS RESCUE FROM SHIPWRECK

IN 1914 THE CHURCH WAS FIRED BY SUFFRAGETTES.

SPOTT P. CHURCH EAST LOTHIAN

THIS MODEST LITTLE CHURCH ON THE T PLAN WITH HAY FAMILY BURIAL AISLE, HAS A GATE WATCH HOUSE BUILT AGAINST THEN RESURRECTIONISTS.

COVENANTORS WERE BURIED HERE & FALLEN AT BATTLE OF DUNBAR.

WATCH HOUSE

BAPTISMAL FONT

A CROWDED PAGE? YES! BUT HOW TO CHOOSE FROM SUCH A WEALTH OF MEANINGFUL PARISH CHURCHES? GIFFORD, MORHAM, GARVALD, PENCAITLAND ETC? HAD TO BE OMITTED

SEE KINEFF CHURCH ON PAGE 11

Dear Nancy,
I know you have
barely 2 days in Edinburgh
on your way N. As a first time
visitor you'll see the Castle of course,
& look down on to Princes St northwards, &
across to Heriot's School & Pentland Hills to the S,
& then walk the historic Royal Mile.

I know you'll want to achieve the climb up on to
Arthur's Seat, but should time or weather prohibit
at least get up the Scott Monument its well worth effort.

On your return from the North,
do get Esther to show you Dalmeny
church after crossing the Forth Bridge,
it will remind you of Kilpeck. Then once
in the city, note that splendid flamboyant edifice
Donaldson's School, a palatial frontage
flaunting its brave panache of towers & turrets.
Did you know John Watson's School is now the Gallery of Modern Art?
SEE PAGE 19 ALSO

Then turn down into
DEAN VILLAGE.
You'll not regret the diversion,
& next visit try to get to
ROSLIN CHAPEL
a remarkably rich
enthralling conception.
You'll have seen notes on these
& much else in "PEN PORTRAITS OF EDINB." &
I know you will pledge yourself to
COME AGAIN
Best wishes to all 3 of you
from
Doris Ann

EDINBURGH'S SKI SLOPE AT HILL END PARK

THESE DANCERS ALWAYS FILL ME WITH JOY

22 GOLF COURSES IN EDINBURGH

ANGELS DO ALSO

REMINDS OF LEUCHARS & TYNINGHAME

CAT ON RED TILE ROOF, RAMSAY GARDEN

GREYFRIARS BOBBY

CARVING FOR MOOR R. MILE

ROSSLYN CHAPEL 1446

BAGPIPE ANGEL

ANGEL WITH TRUMPET

SO ENCRUSTED WITH RICH DECORATION IS THIS REMARKABLE CHAPEL THAT IT LEAVES ME GAZING IN SPEECHLESS CONTEMPLATION OF THE INTRICATE WORKMANSHIP.
I ALMOST WISH I HAD BEEN A MEDIEVAL SCULPTOR !

"THIS SIMPLE, SECLUDED & OFF THE MAP" VILLAGE CHURCH C12, NORMAN, FIGURED PORTAL, SMALL, INTIMATE, WILL I KNOW BE A JOY TO YOU IN PARTICULAR. DALMENY CHURCH

GALLERY OF MODERN ART

TWO OF THE MANY SCULPTURES

PRODIGAL SON & HIS MOTHER [G. ERLICH 1897-1966] IN BRONZE

THE LAMENT LIGNUM VITAE BY BENNO SCHOTZ 1881-

ST GILES

TOLBOOTH, CANONGATE

HUNTLY HOUSE MUSEUM

DO NOTICE THIS JOLLIEST OF SIGNS IN THE ROYAL MILE, CANONGATE.

DONALDSON'S SCHOOL 1854

UNTIL 1969 THE ROYAL HIGH SCHOOL, FOUNDED 1128

APPROACHING FROM THE W, THESE 24? DOMED TURRETS FILL ME WITH JOY

SHAMEFULLY I OMITTED THIS "GREEK TEMPLE" FROM MY PAGE ON SCHOOLS.

"There architecture's noble pride, Bids elegance and splendour rise"

A LOOK AT E·COAST FISHING VILLAGES

"THE FOAM FLOWERS ENDURE WHEN THE ROSE BLOSSOMS WITHER" SWINBURNE

PENNAN, MORAY FIRTH.
5·6·85

That little cottage tucked away into cliff with its tiny bridge over racing burn, was a glamorous surprise. "Chilly today" said its owner "84° F yesterday. We sweltered". [Crovie is exciting too.]

Dear Joan,
I'm so glad to have joined THE STUDY TOUR of E·COAST FISHING VILLAGES BY EDINB. UNIV. EXTRA MURAL STUDIES. 3·6·85

I was peeping into the world of Fisher Folk for the first time, and feeling slightly bewildered being much of a greenhorn, yet was definitely allured by the whole gamut of the trade.

EYEMOUTH. BERWICKSHIRE
BUSTLE ON THE QUAY BUT RAIN & DRIZZLE, RAIN, & SHOWERS RAIN, & MIST WHAT WEATHER 1985
21·6·85 DECGER

Eyemouth was a jostle of boats, & forest of masts today when I roamed river & harbour. The Museum Tapestry, sadly highlighted that fishing disaster 104 yrs ago in 1881.

ISLE OF MAY
N.B. LAW BASS ROCK FIRTH OF FORTH
10·9·85

CRAIL HARBOUR
An evening walk gave me this unusual view of the most picturesque & photoed harbour of this delightful favoured village, full of elements which please. On Bulwarks met Q.W. now in Barbican. Was sorry to miss Truda & Jean.

PITTENWEEM 8·9·85

THICK SUBSTANTIAL SEA WALLS!!

The sea walk past cottages to St Monans has enchantment. I chatted to cottagers. Busy harbour jampacked with boats this Sunday as I scouted around. All disappear tomorrow. to Anstruther.

ST. MONANS 9·9·85
8·9·85

Could there ever be a more romantically sited church? 3 times I rounded it, savouring its charm with burn entering sea. I recalled: FORSAKEN MERMAN "The little grey church on the windy shore".

The responsive enthusiasm of our group knew no bounds, would you agree? Museums all along the route fascinated. ANSTRUTHER MUS. covered a specially wide field. [Zulus, Fifies, Scaffies, Drifters; seine & purse nets etc stories re customs, superstitions, forbidden words we met]

THESE COPIES OF MY RAPID SKETCHES [WHICH REDUCED] CAN GIVE NO FRACTION OF THE CHARM OF THESE FISHING VILLAGE WHICH DESERVE LARGE, DETAILED, DRAWINGS.

ST. ABBS
8·10·85

Thoughts of Cornwall in this homely little harbour [with lifeboat] A joy to behold, under the red sandstone cliffs of St ABBS Head— lighthouse too. Many picnics enjoyed here.

The salt, tangy air, [though chilly] & superb scenery, pepped us all into eager activity. I'll not forget the flowery cliffs as we dropped steeply down into the nooks of sheltered harbours; rock gardens of prize blooms hung in the cliffs.

Walking the formidable breakwaters & bulwarks against a belting wind,
※ SEE "GLIMPSES OF CITIES & COUNTRYSIDES AT HOME & ABROAD by DAG.

ABERDEEN ※

The Round House POCCRA QUAY Pilots' H·Q· Harbour Board with the houses of FITTIE beyond. This [19 planned Fishers' village has cottages facing its 3 squares.
5·5·83

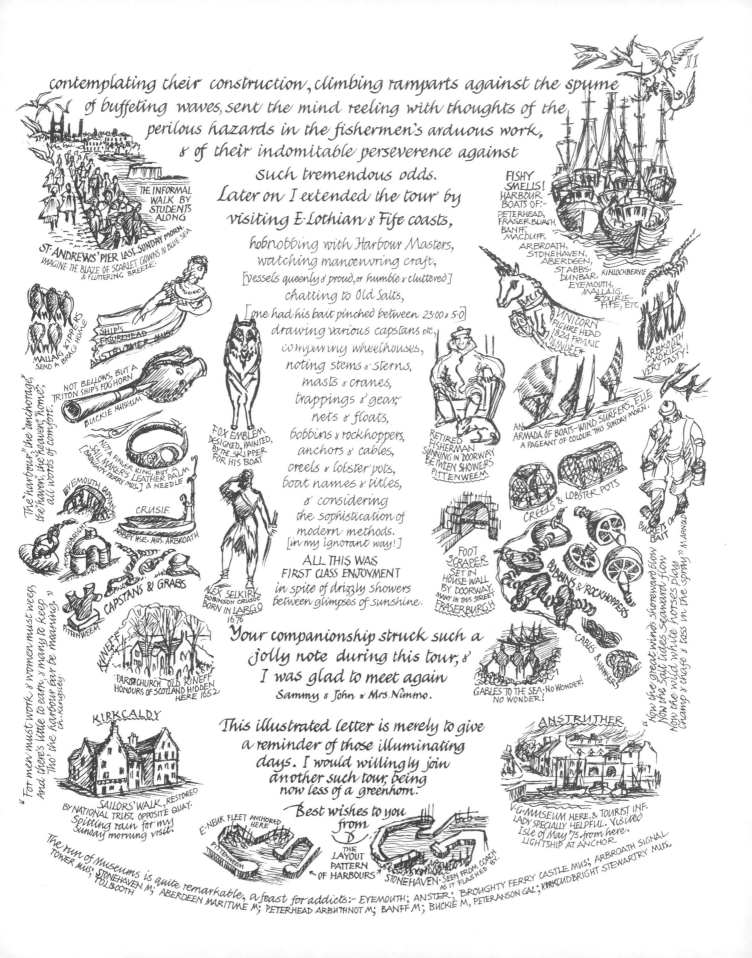

contemplating their construction, climbing ramparts against the spume of buffeting waves, sent the mind reeling with thoughts of the perilous hazards in the fishermen's arduous work, & of their indomitable perseverence against such tremendous odds.

Later on I extended the tour by visiting E. Lothian & Fife coasts,

hobnobbing with Harbour Masters, watching manoeuvring craft, [vessels queenly & proud, or humble & cluttered] chatting to Old Salts, [one had his bait pinched between 23:00 & 5:0] drawing various capstans etc., comparing wheelhouses, noting stems & sterns, masts & cranes, trappings & gear, nets & floats, bobbins & rockhoppers, anchors & cables, creels & lobster pots, boat names & titles, & considering the sophistication of modern methods. [in my ignorant way!]

ALL THIS WAS FIRST CLASS ENJOYMENT in spite of drizzly showers between glimpses of sunshine.

Your companionship struck such a jolly note during this tour, & I was glad to meet again Sammy & John & Mrs. Nimmo.

This illustrated letter is merely to give a reminder of those illuminating days. I would willingly join another such tour, being now less of a greenhorn.

Best wishes to you from D

THE INFORMAL WALK BY STUDENTS ALONG ST. ANDREWS' PIER LAST SUNDAY MORN. IMAGINE THE BLAZE OF SCARLET GOWNS & BLUE SEA & FLUTTERING BREEZE.

MALLAIG KIPPERS SEND A BRAG HOME

SHIP'S FIGUREHEAD ANSTRUTHER MUS.

NOT BELLOWS, BUT A TRITON SHIP'S FOG HORN. BUCKIE MUSEUM

NOT A FINER RING, BUT A SAILMAKER'S LEATHER PALM [BROUGHTY FERRY MUS.] & NEEDLE

EYEMOUTH HARBOUR

CRUSIE. ABBEY HSE. MUS. ARBROATH

KIRKCUDBRIGHT

CAPSTANS & GRABS PITTENWEEM

FOX EMBLEM DESIGNED, PAINTED, BY THE SKIPPER FOR HIS BOAT

ALEX SELKIRK ROBINSON CRUSOE BORN IN LARGO 1676

KINEFF "PARISH CHURCH OLD KINEFF HONOURS OF SCOTLAND HIDDEN HERE 1652

"The 'harbour' the 'anchorage', the 'haven', the 'heaven', 'home', all words of comfort."

"For men must work, & women must weep, And there's little to earn, & many to keep Tho' the harbour bar be moaning." Ch. Kingsley.

FISHY SMELLS! HARBOUR BOATS OF:- PETERHEAD, FRASERBURGH, BANFF, MACDUFF, ARBROATH, STONEHAVEN, ABERDEEN, STABBS, KINLOCHBERVIE DUNBAR, EYEMOUTH, MALLAIG, SCOURIE, FIFE, ETC

UNICORN FIGUREHEAD 1824 FRIGATE IN DUNDEE

ARBROATH 'SMOKIES' VERY TASTY!

RETIRED FISHERMAN SUNNING IN DOORWAY BETWEEN SHOWERS PITTENWEEM

AN ARMADA OF BOATS-WIND SURFERS, ELIE A PAGEANT OF COLOUR THIS SUNDAY MORN.

CREELS & LOBSTER POTS

BUCKETS OF BAIT

FOOT SCRAPER SET IN HOUSE WALL BY DOORWAY. MANY IN THIS STREET FRASERBURGH

BOBBINS & ROCKHOPPERS

CABLES & HAWSERS

GABLES TO THE SEA; NO WONDER! NO WONDER!

"Now the great wind shoreward blow Now the salt tides seaward flow Now the wild white horses play Champ & chafe & toss in the spray" M. Arnold

KIRKCALDY SAILORS' WALK, RESTORED BY NATIONAL TRUST. OPPOSITE QUAY. Spitting rain for my Sunday morning visit.

E. NEUK FLEET ANCHORED HERE PITTENWEEM

THE LAYOUT PATTERN OF HARBOURS

STONEHAVEN - SEEN FROM COACH AS IT FLASHED BY.

ANSTRUTHER

V.G. MUSEUM HERE, & TOURIST INF. LADY SPECIALLY HELPFUL. VISITED Isle of May '75 from here. LIGHTSHIP AT ANCHOR

The run of museums is quite remarkable, a feast for addicts:- EYEMOUTH; ANSTER; BROUGHTY FERRY CASTLE MUS; ARBROATH SIGNAL TOWER MUS; STONEHAVEN M; ABERDEEN MARITIME M; PETERHEAD ARBUTHNOT M; BANFF M; BUCKIE M, PETERANSON GAL; KIRKCUDBRIGHT STEWARTRY MUS. TOLBOOTH

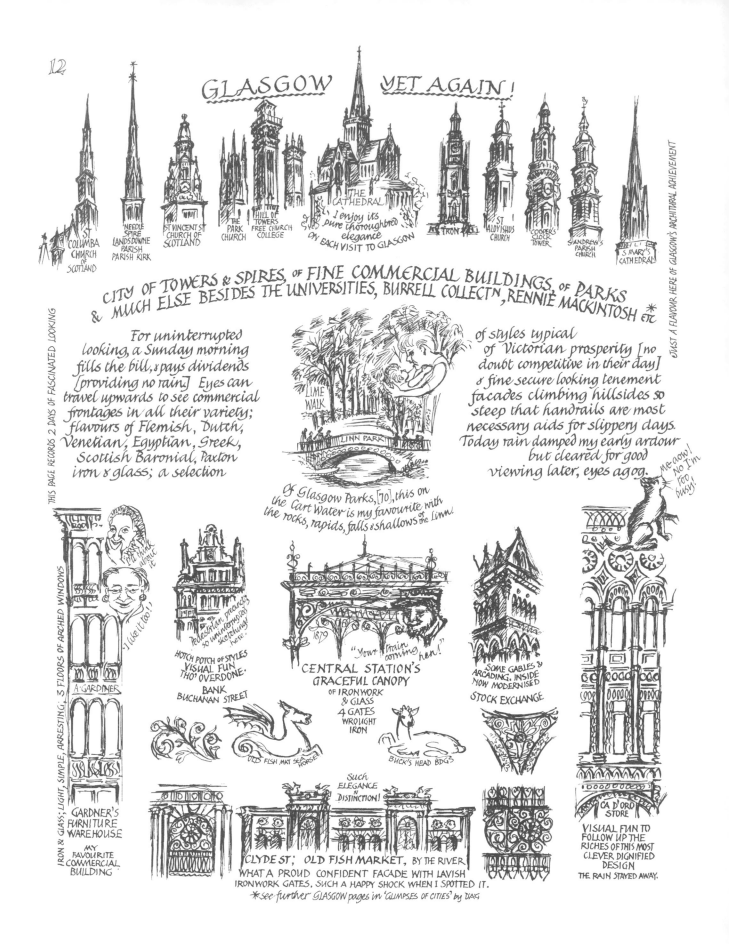

GLASGOW YET AGAIN!

ST COLUMBA CHURCH OF SCOTLAND · **NEEDLE SPIRE LANDSDOWNE PARISH KIRK** · **ST VINCENT ST CHURCH OF SCOTLAND** · **THE PARK CHURCH** · **HILL OF TOWERS FREE CHURCH COLLEGE** · **THE CATHEDRAL** *I enjoy its pure thoroughbred elegance ON EACH VISIT TO GLASGOW* · **ST IRON** · **ST ALOYISHUS CHURCH** · **COOPER'S CLOCK TOWER** · **S ANDREW'S PARISH CHURCH** · **S MARY'S CATHEDRAL**

JUST A FLAVOUR HERE OF GLASGOW'S ARCHITURAL ACHIEVEMENT

CITY OF TOWERS & SPIRES, OF FINE COMMERCIAL BUILDINGS, OF PARKS & MUCH ELSE BESIDES THE UNIVERSITIES, BURRELL COLLECT'N, RENNIE MACKINTOSH etc *

THIS PAGE RECORDS 2 DAYS OF FASCINATED LOOKING

For uninterrupted looking, a Sunday morning fills the bill, & pays dividends [providing no rain] Eyes can travel upwards to see commercial frontages in all their variety; flavours of Flemish, Dutch, Venetian, Egyptian, Greek, Scottish Baronial, Paxton iron & glass; a selection

of styles typical of Victorian prosperity [no doubt competitive in their day] & fine secure looking tenement facades climbing hillsides so steep that handrails are most necessary aids for slippery days. Today rain damped my early ardour but cleared for good viewing later, eyes agog.

meaow! No I'm too busy!

LIME WALK · **LINN PARK**

Of Glasgow Parks, [70], this on the Cart Water is my favourite with the rocks, rapids, falls & shallows the Linn.

IRON & GLASS; LIGHT, SIMPLE, ARRESTING; 3 FLOORS OF ARCHED WINDOWS

I'll think about it · *I like it too!*

A. GARDINER

GARDNER'S FURNITURE WAREHOUSE · MY FAVOURITE COMMERCIAL BUILDING

Pedestrian precincts so uninterrupted sketching here.

HOTCH POTCH OF STYLES VISUAL FUN THO' OVERDONE. **BANK BUCHANAN STREET**

1879 · "Your train coming hen!" · **CENTRAL STATION'S GRACEFUL CANOPY** OF IRONWORK & GLASS 4 GATES WROUGHT IRON

OLD FISH MKT SEA HORSE · BUCK'S HEAD BDGS

SOME GABLES & ARCADING. INSIDE NOW MODERNISED **STOCK EXCHANGE**

CA D'ORO STORE VISUAL FUN TO FOLLOW UP THE RICHES OF THIS MOST CLEVER DIGNIFIED DESIGN THE RAIN STAYED AWAY.

Such ELEGANCE & DISTINCTION!

CLYDE ST; OLD FISH MARKET, BY THE RIVER WHAT A PROUD CONFIDENT FACADE WITH LAVISH IRONWORK GATES, SUCH A HAPPY SHOCK WHEN I SPOTTED IT.

*see further GLASGOW pages in 'GLIMPSES OF CITIES' by DIAS

YET AGAIN GLASGOW

Two-Humped, Lumpy Camelious Camels; Relaxed & Streamlined Lions; extraordinary humps! Humph. Zoo Gdns on hillside above valley. In Calderpark

A HOT JULY CLIMB, BUT I ENJOYED NIPPING DOWN THESE 3 GRANITE FLIGHTS LEADING QUICKLY FROM PARK GARDENS ON HILL, DOWN TO CLAREMONT AND TO SAUCHIEHALL'S!

Each sketch, however crude, records moments of intense joy these two days.

STEWART FOUNTAIN
In Kelvingrove Park, captivating statues in plenty, steep slopes for roly poly, & good picnic spots above the Kelvin.
Sunlight stimulates the pen.
Sunlight I mostly had, & peach picnic.

SCULPTURE KELVINGROVE PARK How nobly depicted!

BRIDGETON CROSS
The 'UMBRELLA' as it is locally called strikes the gayest note; on my visit today it was a sunshade to folk sitting around.
Avocado picnic for me.
GREETINGS TO SUSAN C, KAY B, KATE J, MARG K & FRANCES S.
She persisted in following me into Buchanan St.

THE PEOPLES PALACE MUSEUM & WINTER GDN ON GLASGOW GREEN BY THE CLYDE I much enjoy this setting

JAS MARTIN 1895
THIS DREAM OF A FOUNTAIN HAD TO BE DRAWN WITHIN AND WITHOUT, EYES STARRY WITH PLEASURE ALL OF THE TIME. WHAT CRAFTMANSHIP!
What expertise from workers!
On Glasgow Green
McFarlane's Foundry

"Works done least rapidly Art most cherishes," said RBG Do you agree?
BUCHANAN ST's PEDESTRIAN PRECINCT BUT NO ROOM TO DRAW ARGYLL ARCADE

ST. ANDREW'S cast iron suspension foot bridge, across the Clyde from Bridgeton to Glasgow Green.

MUSONIUS, PHILOSOPHER SAYS:- [N. GRIMALD 1540]
"In working, if travail you sustain, Into the wind shall lightly pass the pain; But of the deed, the glory shall remain."

A wet day? Many hours can be spent happily in the various Galleries, Museums, Libraries.
Sun appearing? Make for those many Parks, the Clyde, the Hills, & Countryside
LET GLASGOW FLOURISH
* MORE GLASGOW PAGES TO BE SEEN IN "GLIMPSES OF CITIES" by DAG.

NOTES ON A FEW OF OUR FAVOURITE HILLS

THE 1½ ML RIDGE   THE THIMBLE   THE OBELISK   THE AIGUILLES

FROM CANISP   FROM LOCHINVER   FROM STRATH OYKELL   FROM N & S

One of the most exciting & sudden views I know, opens at Craggie, by the head of Strath Oykell, when above the billowing gneiss landscape of Assynt, the sandstone peaks bob up, each separate one towering mightily in its grand isolation. WHICH WOULD WE CLIMB? ✳

My most astonishing peak is SUILVEN, astonishing because of its many profiles like the changing expressions of a well kent face. Thus it so clearly gives the compass points. WE NEVER ACHIEVED THE PEAK. ✳

"It rose, dark as a stack of peat with mountains at its feet, Till a bright flush of evening swept And on to its high shoulder leapt And Suilven, a great ruby, shone." Andrew Young.

"NEVER DID SUN MORE BEAUTIFULLY STEEP IN HIS FIRST SPLENDOUR VALLEY ROCK AND HILL" W.W.

PEAKS, FIRST TO GREET THE DAWN, LAST TO LOSE THE SUNSET

STAC POLLY 2009

A single isolated peak, a favourite of mine, & of many a country walker. Frightening neither to young nor old, nor to town addicts. Climb with joy, picking your route to the rapturous coxcomb peak of bristling pinnacles MAY 1957 APRIL 1960

LEAVETAKING
" Pass thou wild light,
Wild light on peaks that so
Grieve, Grieve to let go the day.
Love thy tarrying, lovely too is night,
Pass thou away." W Watson

To live near a hill is most inspiring. [Edinburgh has seven.] We both recall tremendous encounters with experience & with weathers on:-

Cairn Gorm, Lairig Ghru, Cairn Toul, Brae Riarch, Ben Mac Dhui, [all before the amenity of chair-lifts] Schiehallion, Ben Ledi, Ben Wrackie, Ben Vorlich, Nevis, Eighe, Saddle, the horns of Ben Alligin, Resipol, Cruachan, Blaven, Marsco; all such various characters, these.

A CHIMNEY OF DUN CAAN

✳ Another favourite peak but elusively away on the misty Isle of RAASAY. A cynosure & magnet for years. Miles of ankle twisting moor & bog we negotiated, trackless, then up we clambered to the glorious platform top. SEPT 1966 Views entrancing. Danced, as did Boswell, BrJ 1773.

UNISEX

"May cloud & mountain, lake & vale, Never to you be trite or stale," wrote W Watson to JCM.

"Great things are done when men and mountains meet" wrote W. Blake

"IF THY HEART FAILS THEE" SAID Q. ELIZ I, "CLIMB NOT AT ALL." I SOMETIMES FELT LIKE TAKING THIS ADVICE MYSELF !

Inadequate miniature of LIATHACH, & the mighty steeps of this terraced monarch of Torridon sandstone hills, some with quartzite caps. We twice drove from Diabeg to enjoy fully the magic of its sunset beauty.

Our Balmacara Cottage backed onto a minor hill with major slopes, & gave sunrise climbs with panoramic views; boulders for perch while drawing breath; steeps; screes; cairns; foot baths; tarns; flower starred slopes, & much companionship. ✳

L. CORIUSK, locked away in its mountain fastness. Twice I've been haunted by its aura. "A scene so wild & rude as this Yet so sublime in barreness." W. Scott

GET TO THE TOP! GET TO THE LONELY PLACES! flatter the mountain ---- tops with sovereign eye " W.Sh.

"Full many a glorious morning have I seen

The lilting profile of many peaked, granite, Ben LOYAL, graces & enhances views from all points in Sutherland, a fine range of peaks tho' not lofty. Here I lost my map round skirt, found in its pocket 48 hrs after. ✳

✳ "WESTERN HIGHLANDS & ISLANDS," BY D.A.G REFERS MORE FULLY TO THE ABOVE HILLS, WITH STORIES & VERSES

"And let the misty mountain winds be free
To blow against thee." W.W.

YESNABY CASTLE, ORKNEY

OLD MAN OF HOY

GLOUP, TED. BINGS.

Oh, the peaceful days in Orkney
but the wind! Off Yesnaby
Cliffs it was a merciless monster!
In spite of it, found Primula Scottica!

Granite rockwalls of THE STORR ✱
"Rough quarries, rocks, hills, whose heads touch heaven") OTHELLO

NATURE'S
STONES

PINNACLES
PEAKS
OBELISKS
SPIRES
COLUMNS
CHIMNEYS
STACKS
MONOLITHS
FANGS
TOWERS
CASTLES
SAUCERS
CORRIES
BLOWHOLES

Sanctuary
figures

Grotesque
weirdies
of the
Quirang;
The Needle
Old Man; Prison,
Sanctuary.

skeletal
stark obelisks &
tors rise from
steeply sloping
screes

I was hell bent on getting here, bizarre, macabre,
spooky, withal; & terrifying.

EN FAMILLE

BOW & FIDDLE
PORT KNOCKIE. MET 2 FRIENDLY GERMAN YOUTHS

MACLEOD'S MAIDENS,
IDRIGILL POINT, SKYE, Scott's
"RIDERS OF THE STORM"
All these & countless other
stacks give added
excitement
to cliff
walks ✱

How they excite
the eager.!

How they intrigue
the geologist!

How they provide for
man's physical needs!

How they feed
the contemplative
in moments
of timeless
illumination!

"'Tis pleasant
thru' the loopholes of retreat,
To peep at such a world."
William Cowper 1731-1800

ROCK SLABS OF PEAK,
GOAT FELL, ARRAN. ✱
My first mountain.
WHEW! We're up!
The triumphant
joy of that heady
1st climb in
1928.

GEO STACK
thronging birds &
loud with cries on
HANDA ISLAND.
[a pen active day!]

SPOTTED
WITH
BINOCS,
CARLIN
MAGGIE, BASALT
COLUMN 40' ON
W. SIDE OF WEST
LOMOND HILL
FIFE.

NATURE'S STONES FASHIONED BY MAN

"E'er the parting hour go by, Quick, thy tablets, Memory!" To his Friends, MATT. ARNOLD

KILMARTIN 10. APRIL
I found
this weathered
remnant most
moving.

KILDALTON
ISLAY
Out
in one
stone

ROUND
TOWER
BRECHIN
Nan [Montrose]
was keen
for us to see this
Viking Tower.
In Ireland used
as refuges.

CLACKMANNAN.
THE OLD TOLBOOTH, endearingly striking
to me [but not to others in former days!]
Belfry Clock Tower, Town Cross, & Stone of Manau

"Bridging the gulf of countless days
We have knit the near and the far."

STIRLING
OLD BRIDGE

FOOT
BRIDGE
ONLY

BULLARS OF BUCHAN
BOILERS

The treacherous complicated
nature of these eroded
sea cliffs cannot be
compressed into a square
inch! Given a fine day with
sea pink cushions & red campion,
they are a geo thrill

Drawing this ancient bridge I was transported back thro'
the centuries, though conscious of contemporary pram wheels on the
cobbles.
✱ SEE 'HIGHLAND & ISLAND DAYS' by D.A.G.

16

STIRLING

A CROWDING OF MEMORIES FROM GALLOWAY & AROUND.

"Let's make acquaintance with the S.W." We set out for our 1st visit from Haddington, for this extensive triangle at 4:30 a.m. June '54, pausing for a rapturous sunrise across Broughton heights, & made our zig-zag way to Dumfries, *lost sketch book for 5 whole hours!* A keen appetite for further roving visits '70, '74, '85, brought us to Leadhills, Sanquhar, Moniaive, Drumlanrig, Dalry, Newton Stewart, Bowhill, Kirkcudbright & so on. *seeing much missing a bit!* GALLOWAY WAS NEW TO ME IN 1954. FELT I WANTED TO DRAW EACH NOOK & CORNER!

BLACK SMITH HAD FUN. DAUGHTER ON WALL

KIRKCUDBRIGHT TOLBOOTH HAS SCHOONER WINDVANE, JOUGS, & TOWN CROSS.

IN SKIRLING, UNUSUAL IRONWORK IN TINY VILLAGE, & CHURCH GATES VERY DECORATIVE. deserted village! Not a soul about

HAVE LOST MY SKETCH OF THE CADGERS' BRIG. BIGGAR

TINY BURN FOOTBRIDGE VERY WELL USED. AVOCADO PICNIC HERE. memory

OLD INKWELLS [SWAN] IN BIGGAR MUSEUM

BIGGAR'S church has a hill setting above the burn, & the Museum is an achievement

Charmed by the quiet pastoral countryside, we went wayfaring on, attracted here & there by homesteads, gardens, abbeys, castles, & of course by friends, & friends of friends.

From Girvan south to THE RHINNS, & LOGAN & MULL OF GALLOWAY; Ireland to W, Isle of Man to S; but alas we were shrouded in bright mist. "It's lifting" said a shadow "just wait" We did. A misty plum picnic; then slowly, glimmers of sun.

LADY GIFFORD CLOCK TOWER
GRAVESTONE, CHURCHYARD,
WEST LINTON 9.0.am

'85 I succumbed to the charms of KIRKCUDBRIGHT; took ham salad picnic on the shore; scallop & lobster fishing boats; enjoyed the Stewartry Museum; drew the Tolbooth & Cross; walked the park & hillside for graveyard yett. Chatted with native who had good sense of humour as well as civic pride. We sipped sherry with laughter, outside his door.

THE PASTORAL COUNTRYSIDE SO PLEASED, THAT WE PITCHED BY A MEADOW BURN & MADE A LITTLE HOME FOR 2 BALMY NIGHTS. "And flower lulled in sleepy grass, I hear the cool lapse of hours pass." R. Brooke.

Ravenshall Cliffs smothered with primroses April '54. found hare's nest, clutch of speckled eggs & much else besides silver coins. BUT LENT my ducky little diary, & have never seen it since.

FERRYING STONES

Carved stone, on house in New Abbey village, of the 3 women who helped Devorgilla build her Abbey 1273, where she was buried plus the heart of her husband; thus the Abbey's name, 'Sweetheart'. Our visit was not long enough. I want a holiday in this little village on the Pow Burn backed by Criffel. No room to draw Cardoness Castle which lay on our route.

SWEETHEART CISTERCIAN ABBEY 1273

GATEHOUSE OF FLEET CLOCK TOWER TO THE TOP HEAVY LOOKING. Scott, Burns, & Sayers here

MERRICK A morning walk up 2764'. Stone added to cairn. Grey man spotted, then down to picnic [cauliflower] in GLEN TROOL!

ADAM & EVE STONE
MOORE'S KING & QUEEN They took some finding, out on the moor, Glenkiln. I met Henry while these figures were being worked.

From DALRY we drove to KELLS churchyard to see this; the Covenanter's Grave 1685; & other carved stones. Oh! those brave Covenanters!

WATER MOAT. ROUGH IDEA OF PLAN 13
CAERLAVEROCK CASTLE I was keen to see this, on triangular plan; towered gateway, Maxwell crest Renaissance facade.

The busy footbridge over the R. Nith, links Dumfries with Maxwelltown. Athletic divers had just completed their swims, & I my sketch, before sudden rain pelted.

MID STEEPLE DUMFRIES The enemy hastened this sketch too — an April day in July! So, visited Museum & Burns House with much contemplation

"How fled the vacant solitary hours, By dancing rivulet & silent pool." Chris North

AN ALLURING QUIET COUNTRYSIDE OF RURAL SCENES & SEASCAPES, CASTLES, TOWNS, VILLAGES, WINDING RIVERS. "And this our life, exempt from public haunt, Finds tongues in trees, books in the running brooks, Sermons in stones, & good in everything." W.Sh.

MELROSE.
The name alone charms, as does its individual features;- THE ABBEY, stirring, exclusive, its carvings & lawns; the flower gardens; river walk; apple orchard; exhibitions. [I was glad of my pocket binoculars.] Abbotsford near by; thoughts of Scott & Hogg the Ettrick Shepherd; & St Mary's Loch not far off.

& reap the rich rewards, Glen Sax is one

SCULPTURE IN APPLE GARDEN

The lilting line of the EILDONS [TRIMONTIUM] epitomises the Borders for me. Lovely from all angles, but 'Scott's View is choice, as he, & his horse, **knew well**.

"Three crests against the saffron sky
Beyond the purple plain,
The kind remembered melody
Of Tweed will e'er remain." A. LANG.

"Ah, Tam! Gie me a Border burn
Which canna rin without a turn." J.B.S.

THE WINDING RIVER TWEED, LOVED, FISHED, & SUNG BY CONTEMPLATIVES THROUGHOUT THE CENTURIES.

DRYBURGH ABBEY.
In its pastoral R. Tweed setting, the lyric beauty of columns & arcades rises above buttercup meadows, or springtime banks of snowdrops & aconites or daffodils.

order of your going, But Go!"

For a gentle steady walk try TINTO 2335 & add your stone to the tall cairn. Our sunny date was 4.5.73 DAG MJ KS.
"The air is full of ballad notes
Born out of long ago." A. Lang.

MOFFAT'S RAM.
So transfixed was I by this powerful sculpture that the specialities of the Toffee Shop nearly eluded me!

RUBER'S LAW, another kindly hill for savouring the sweet Border air, with a shepherd for local companionship.
"Come forth and bring with you a heart That watches and receives." W.W.

1392

JEDBURGH ABBEY

On each of 3 visits I've been captivated by this masterpiece, the ABBEY, in red sandstone, & sheer beauty of the long nave. A long informative chat with local farmer before visiting Queen Mary's House.

GREY MARE'S TAIL WATER FALL 200'.... FROM LOCH SKENE, TAIL BURN JOINS MOFFAT WATER & RUSHES TO MOFFAT

CLIMB EITHER SIDE OF THE RAVINE FOR VIEWS WHICH ARE SPEC-TAC-U-LAR! THEN CAMP BELOW.

In KELSO I looked across from lovely Tweedside walks, to Abbey gables topping tall trees, & towards the long lines of Floors Castle.

WELL QUAY RIVER WALKS

Have you been ???

"Stand not upon the

SELKIRK, on sloping hillside above the Ettrick Water. July heat; ice cream; then thunderstorm prevented further exploration, so read in Library, Mungo Park.

WAS DELIGHTED TO MEET E. AITKENHEAD AGAIN

THE BORDERS ARE THE EPITOME OF GENTLY PERSUASIVE UPLAND COUNTRY. ITS GREEN HUMPS, LUMPS, BUMPS; ITS FOLDS, PEAKS; ITS VALES, RIVERS, BURNS, LOCHS; ITS WOODLANDS & PASTURES; ALL IN CLOSE PROXIMITY COMBINE TO PRESENT THE CHARM WHICH LIES HERE.

"And around the dear ruin each wish of my heart, Would entwine itself verdantly still." T. Moore 1779 -1852

ST MARY'S LOCH SHOULD NOT BE MISSED.

THE PEEBLES BRIDGE ON THE ALLURING MUCH LOVED TWEED, THE BRIDGE CROSSING TO THE TOWN, KNOWN FOR INDIVIDUAL CHARM; ITS SHOPS, RIVER WALKS, ETC.

From the South, after the long climb up to Carter Bar, whew! what a view! The Border Hills bathed in spectacular beauty, verdant, rolling. "As well as seeing Abbeys, WE MUST CLIMB THESE HILLS FOR SUNRISE BREAKFASTS, & SUNSET PANORAMIC COFFEES," we both agreed. 3 times MMB & I breakfasted from Haddington on the Eildons

SOME OF SCOTLAND'S PALACES

WROTE JOUBERT IN 1790:—
"You will not find poetry anywhere
unless you bring some of it with you"

TO LINLITHGOW
WITH J· FEBRUARY 25 1985

BITTER COLD; STILL;
NOT A MOUSE STIRRING!

We brought plenty in our exploration of the vast shell of LINLITHGOW PALACE. It sent our imaginations soaring. We were uplifted, & took the 150 steps [in each of 4 corners the central turnpike stairs] with winged feet. 'Walls have hearsay' is said, & these spoke to us of Kings, Queens, Nobles, retinues, rich tapestries & sculptures. J. aged 11, a romantic historian, glowed with interest, & peopled these spacious chambers & halls with costumed figures. I drew with zest, pocket warmer a comfort, BUT FEET LIKE SLABS OF ICE!

FOUNTAIN
SCULPTURED
FIGURES

WEATHER
BEATEN

Palace
once richly
sculptured
with niche
figures.
Remnants, [difficult to see] now
ravaged by
time.

FIVE STOREYS

We
revelled
in these
well
lighted
Turnpike
(wheel)
stairways.
Look up, look
down, how very
beautiful
they are.

FOUNTAIN BY
K· JAMES V IN
THE CLOSE.

A similar elaborate
fountain in the Palace
forecourt of Holyrood House,
was erected by Q· Victoria

CURIOUS
14-LIGHT
WINDOW
INNER
CLOSE

A most exciting
WALL WALK

"THE
UTTER
GRET BULWARK"
FLYING BUTTRESSES
TWO ROUND TOWERS
& SMALL STAIR TOWER

A beautiful setting on green slopes high above the loch; boats, swans, duck.

from MARMION W. Scott:—
"Of all the Palaces so fair
Built for the Royal dwelling
In Scotland, far beyond compare
Linlithgow is excelling."

JAMES I BUILT IT; SUCCESSIVE KINGS IMPROVED IT; MARY, Q. OF SCOTS & JAMES V WERE BORN IN IT.

FALKLAND
PALACE
FIFE

1537

TWIN
TOWERS
OF ENTRANCE
GATE HOUSE

Falkland Palace,
'Hunting Box' of the Stuarts who
stayed or visited here under the
Lomond ridges for their sport &
relaxation [falconland?] See the South
Wing French style façade, & 1539 Tennis Court, then
enjoy this picturesque Royal Burgh with
its cobbled streets, old houses, & Town House spire.

DUNFERMLINE PALACE
once existed, but now little evidence remains save
a buttressed wall & a remnant of Malcolm's Tower.

"The King sits in Dunfermline toune
Drinking the blude-reid wine
'O whar will I get a guid sailor,
To sail this schip of mine?'"
[BALLAD:— SIR PATRICK SPENS]

KIRKWALL
ORKNEY

EARL'S
PALACE
ORKNEY

Two of the fine
corbelled windows of
this "most accomplished Eliz.
ruin". I was happily astonished
at such Renaissance splendour here
in Orkney, & perilously climbed the
narrow parapets. Trees? Yes! Unbelievably.
Great leafy sycamores next the Bishop's Palace.

THE LOMOND HILLS
OF FIFE

THE CHURCHILL "BOULDER"
BARRIERS SCAPA FLOW ORKNEY

CASTLE HILL

ARTHURS SEAT

CALTON HILL

WROTE R. FERGUSSON:-

CROWNED THISTLE LAMP, ONE OF SOME 5 OR MORE, V. SIMILAR.

ROYAL CROWN OF CENTRAL CUPOLA. CLOCK DATED 1680

"Let me to Arthur's seat pursue
Whare bonny pastures meet the view;
Or should some cankered biling show'r
The day and all her sweets devour
To Holyrood House let me then stray
And gie to musing a' the day."

THE PALACE OF
HOLYROOD HOUSE

JEWELLED POWDER HORN GOLD MOUNTS

Now that we're retired to Haddington from London (with Buckingham Palace not far away) we agreed straightway to pay our respects to Edinburgh by visiting the near by Palace of Holyrood House. We chose to go in midwinter, no queues, small groups & a more intimate & responsive note in the guide's recited narrations.

SEGMENTED SILVER POMANDER
one of many visits
MARY Q of SCOTS 4cms diameter

As well as hand moulded plaster ceilings; fine tapestries; [of Diana the huntress and children playing;] furniture; & the layout of this C17 House, small attractions were:- Mary Q of Scots' exquisite silver pomander, her 'cat & mouse' embroidery & work box top, the jewelled powder horn, & engraved Jacobean glass.

TOURISTS

This city of Edinburgh sprouts exciting hills within its boundary;- Castle Hill, the tourists' mecca; Arthur's Seat, the May Day venue; Blackford Hill (the Astronomer Royal;) Calton Hill, beloved of R.L. Stevenson; Braid Hills, beloved of Golfers; The Pentlands, adored by generations of devotees, literary folk, artists, figures eminent in many fields; & plain walkers like us.

GUIDE

ENGRAVED SPIRAL STEM WINE GLASS
JACOBEAN

And here at the foot of the Royal Mile, a stone's throw from Arthur's Seat, the Firth of Forth hard by, the railway at its side, steaming breweries in front, stands The Palace, surely by location alone quite in a class of its own.

EMBROIDERY BY MARY Q. SCOTS

SEE ALSO "PEN PORTRAITS OF EDINBURGH - by DAR

IN JULY
IN FEB.

SCONE PALACE

YOUNG BRACKEN FRONDS

"As thus we talked our barge did sweetly pass
By Scone's fair Palace, sometime Abbey was—
But Palace fair which doth so richly stand
With gardens, orchids, parks on either hand"
Henry C17 Adamson

The romance of Scone [Abbey & Palace] fascinated me, so I first sought tree clad Moot Hill where Scottish Kings were crowned until Ch II. [The story goes that chiefs would fill their boots with their own soil, stand on Moot Hill swearing allegiance, as on their own land, then empty their boots!] This ancient Abbey site was Scotland's Westminster & here was the Royal Seat, the STONE OF DESTINY until Edw Ist took it to London in 1296. WHAT A FURORE AT ITS SENSATIONAL DISAPPEARANCE IN 1950!! FOUND IN ARBROATH 1951, REPLACED IN WESTMINSTER ABBEY. After touring the Palace, we sought our erstwhile good neighbours [DONELLY FAMILY] then settled in Scone.

BY BURN & RIVER, TOLBOOTH & TOWN HOUSE.

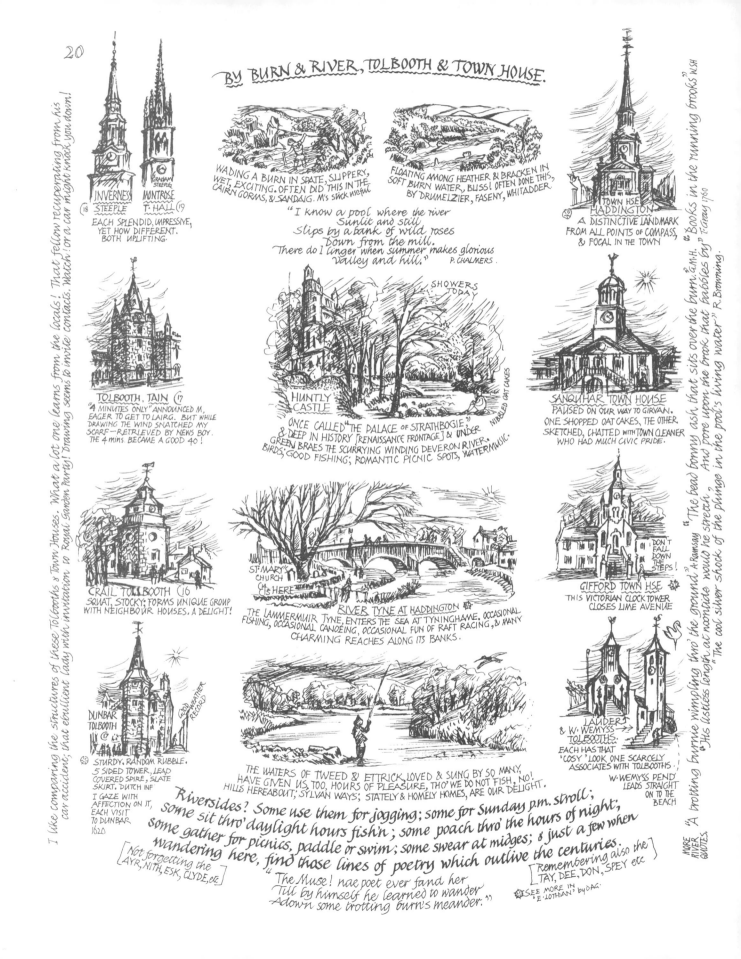

I like comparing the structures of these Tolbooths & Town Houses. What a lot one learns from the locals! That fellow recuperating from his car accident; that ebullient lady with invitation to Royal Garden Party! Drawing seems to invite contacts. Watch! or a car might knock you down!

INVERNESS STEEPLE (18) **MONTROSE T.HALL** (19) [GRAHAM STEEPLE]
EACH SPLENDID, IMPRESSIVE, YET HOW DIFFERENT. BOTH UPLIFTING.

WADING A BURN IN SPATE, SLIPPERY, WET, EXCITING. OFTEN DID THIS IN THE CAIRNGORMS, & SANDAIG. M's STICK USEFUL

FLOATING AMONG HEATHER & BRACKEN IN SOFT BURN WATER, BLISS! OFTEN DONE THIS, BY DRUMELZIER, FASENY, WHITADDER.

"I know a pool where the river
Sunlit and still
Slips by a bank of wild roses
Down from the mill.
There do I linger when summer makes glorious
Valley and hill." P. CHALMERS.

TOWN HSE HADDINGTON
A DISTINCTIVE LANDMARK FROM ALL POINTS OF COMPASS, & FOCAL IN THE TOWN

TOLBOOTH, TAIN (17
"4 MINUTES ONLY" ANNOUNCED M, EAGER TO GET TO LAIRG. BUT WHILE DRAWING THE WIND SNATCHED MY SCARF—RETRIEVED BY NEWS BOY. THE 4 MINS. BECAME A GOOD 40!

SHOWERS TODAY
HUNTLY CASTLE NIBBLED OAT CAKES
ONCE CALLED "THE PALACE OF STRATHBOGIE," & DEEP IN HISTORY [RENAISSANCE FRONTAGE] & UNDER GREEN BRAES THE SCURRYING WINDING DEVERON RIVER. BIRDS, GOOD FISHING; ROMANTIC PICNIC SPOTS, WATERMUSIC.

SANQUHAR TOWN HOUSE
PAUSED ON OUR WAY TO GIRVAN. ONE SHOPPED OAT CAKES, THE OTHER SKETCHED, CHATTED WITH TOWN CLEANER WHO HAD MUCH CIVIC PRIDE.

CRAIL TOLBOOTH (16
SQUAT, STOCKY; FORMS UNIQUE GROUP WITH NEIGHBOUR HOUSES. A DELIGHT!

ST MARY'S CHURCH IS HERE
RIVER TYNE AT HADDINGTON
THE LAMMERMUIR TYNE, ENTERS THE SEA AT TYNINGHAME. OCCASIONAL FISHING, OCCASIONAL CANOEING, OCCASIONAL FUN OF RAFT RACING, & MANY CHARMING REACHES ALONG ITS BANKS.

DON'T FALL DOWN THE STEPS!
GIFFORD TOWN HSE
THIS VICTORIAN CLOCK TOWER CLOSES LIME AVENUE

DUNBAR TOLBOOTH GOOD WEATHER RECORD
STURDY, RANDOM RUBBLE. 5 SIDED TOWER, LEAD COVERED SPIRE, SLATE SKIRT. DUTCH INF
I GAZE WITH AFFECTION ON IT, EACH VISIT TO DUNBAR 1620

THE WATERS OF TWEED & ETTRICK, LOVED & SUNG BY SO MANY, HAVE GIVEN US, TOO, HOURS OF PLEASURE, THO' WE DO NOT FISH, NO! HILLS HEREABOUT, SYLVAN WAYS; STATELY & HOMELY HOMES, ARE OUR DELIGHT.

LAUDER & W. WEMYSS TOLBOOTHS.
EACH HAS THAT 'COSY' LOOK ONE SCARCELY ASSOCIATES WITH TOLBOOTHS.
W. WEMYSS PEND' LEADS STRAIGHT ON TO THE BEACH

Riversides? Some use them for jogging; some for Sunday p.m. stroll; some sit thro' daylight hours fish'n; some poach thro' the hours of night; some gather for picnics, paddle or swim; some swear at midges; & just a few when wandering here, find those lines of poetry which outlive the centuries.

[Not forgetting the AYR, NITH, ESK, CLYDE, etc.]
[Remembering also the TAY, DEE, DON, SPEY etc]

"The Muse! nae poet ever fand her
Till by himself he learned to wander
Adown some trotting burn's meander."

SEE MORE IN E.LOTHIAN by D.A.G.

MORE RIVER QUOTES:
"Books in the running brooks" W.SH.
"The bead bonny ash that sits over the burn." G.M.H.
"The listless length at noontide would he stretch, And pore upon the brook that babbles by." T.Gray 1750
"The cool silver shock of the plunge in the pool's living water." R. Browning.
"A trotting burnie wimpling thro' the ground." A.Ramsay

A MIXTER MAXTER OF MEMORIES

ABERDEEN MERCAT X

This arcaded cross gave me shelter July '83 during sudden downpour

PRESTON MERCAT X

specially appealing for the shell seats I sunbathed in.

BANFF CROSS

Unusual for its figure symbols v. meaningful to me, tho' difficult to see clearly

MUCKLE CROSS ELGIN

I was sketching this platform cross at 22:15 with great pleasure June '85

DUFF HOUSE BANFF

SECOND STAIR

WILL ADAM 1760

Looking down, the perspective of this stair thrilled me

Visited JULY 79

JUNE 1985 with Edinburgh University

ORANGE PICNIC

KILDRUMMY WATER GARDEN
Can almost get lost here in this fertile gorge

Viridian water, azure skies, cerulean meconopsis.
Sheer bliss was this perfect day in ASCRIEVIE GDN with its sheltered lakes.

WITH SCOTTS GDNS TRUST   June '78

ALL THE GARDENS OF TYNINGHAME HOUSE EXCEL

My utter astonishment at discovering this little Norman gem knew no bounds, none. What a choice setting for it. Each visit increases my devotion

RHODOS, ALPINES

U.S.A. FLOWER ENTHUSIASTS BRANKLYN GARDENS PERTH 1985

PEAT GARDEN

98' CLOCK TOWER KIRKCALDY

WEATHER VANE 7½' ST BRYCE N TREE

OF CIVIC CENTRE
GREETINGS TO JUDY & SANGA

ULLAPOOL

TOWN CLOCK   ULLAPOOL

My very rubbed sketch of this; dated Easter '57 with Joy! Memorial Clock 1899.

Why are Scottish gardens so very special? Is it the rainfall? the moist climate? south facing slopes? rocky outcrops? burns? Gulf Stream? Or is it the long light of summer, & Scottish gardener's skill? I recalled:- "All the flare and gusto of the unenduring Joys of a season" L. MC NEICE

Hunting out drawings for this page has been an engaging joyful pastime [tho' TOO MUCH TIME HAS PASSED] Vivid memories have awakened

"When green buds hang in the elm like dust, &sprinkle the lime with rain; Forth I wander, forth I must, And drink of life again" A.E.HOUSMAN 1859-1936

CASTLES

"Do you have castles in Scotland?" asked 7yr old Jon from New Zealand. "Hundreds" I boasted; "on cliffs, (almost in the sky,) on rocky islands, by rivers, above seas, rising up from deep lochs, on rocky shores, many ruined, some inhabited, all exciting."

"I'd like to see them all, every one, can we?" A tall order! (no time sense as yet) (no distance concept?)

So off we went, (Edinburgh of course, in priority) to nibble our way into this rich feast. The local E. Lothian castles followed & so on.

MISGIVING:- WOULD I EVER DEVELOP AN INTEREST IN CASTLES? CONJECTURE:- WOULD HE TIRE OF IT? HOW SOON? THEY SAY GROWN UPS CAN LEARN FROM CHILDREN!

THROUGH THIS LITTLE BOY I BECAME ADDICTED, FINGERED EACH CASTLE HELD ME SPELLBOUND AS I GAZED, FINGERED & FELT ITS CARVED STONES, STUDIED ITS CHEQUERED ANCIENT HISTORY & LONG LIFE. THANK YOU, JON

EDINBURGH CASTLE.

set grandly on its towering rock, looking down on to Princes St Gardens northwards, & the well of Grassmarket to the south. You sense the essence of this mighty fortress as you climb by the protruding lava rock under those massive walls of the Battery, through the Argyll portcullis Tower, & on to reach that climax of views & the rare diminutive gem of C11 Queen Margaret's chapel. Just beyond is the Citadel with its Palace, & the unique impressive & most moving War Memorial. OF COURSE YOU NOTICED MONS MEG, & THE FIRE BASKET Every visit, the tiny chapel of Q. Marg quickens me.

FURTHER DESCRIPTIONS IN "ROYAL MILE GUIDE" & IN "PEN PORTRAITS OF EDINBURGH" BY D·A·G

DUNBAR CASTLE

1338 BRAVE BLACK AGNES! A STIRRING STORY TO RECALL AS YOU CLIMB THESE REMNANTS & BROOD UPON THEIR HISTORY.

LOOKS DOWN ON FISHING BOATS IN HARBOUR

DIRLETON CASTLE C13

A ROUSING EXPERIENCE - a joy for youngsters with its ups & downs dark doorways, maze of cavernous chambers, cells, donjons, lookouts, moat doocot etc. A rocky eminence, a crammed site. Polygonal hall in drum tower, rib vaulted, with 3 embrasures each one seated. Superb lawns, & ancient cypresses & yews round C7 Bowling green.

C15 BUFFET GREAT HALL

I sat, pondering in a C4 dream of trailing gown & steeple head dress!

MORE ABOUT DIRLETON, DUNBAR, TANTALLAN, IN "EAST LOTHIAN" by D·A·G.

HAILES CASTLE · R·TYNE · BY TRAPRAIN LAW · E·LOTHIAN

C13 MASONRY. VAULTED PIT PRISON. HALL· BAKEHOUSE. MARY Q· OF SCOTS HERE ON WAY TO DUNBAR CASTLE (BOTHWELL). SWANS ON RIVER, CROCUS, SNOWDROPS, DAFFS, BY WATERFALLS OF BURN.

TANTALLON CASTLE'S

dramatic setting on cliff outcrop opposite the BASS ROCK. ("THE WRINKLED SEA BENEATH HIM CRAWLS" A.T.) A good wall walk here, well, moat & doocot.

BREEZY? HAAR? WILD WAVES? GANNETS? STIMULATED? PICNIC?

CRICHTON CASTLE C14

8·4·1971 P; Rob, & Katie, romped on the green hillocks sloping down to the young Tyne. [JAN· 1985, A BILLOWING, SUNNY SNOW WHITE LANDSCAPE, NOT A TWIG STIRRING, THRILLING!]

THE OUTSIDE GIVES NO CLUE TO THE ITALIANATE N·WING, THE NAILHEAD DIAMOND FACADE OF ARCADED COURTYARD, THE CORBELLED BALCONY, THE GUN LOOPED HANGING TURRET, BALL & FLOWER CORNICE ENRICHMENT ETC.

"That castle rises on the steep Of the green vale of Tyne; And far beneath where slow they creep From pool to eddy dark & deep, Where alders, moist, & willows weep, You hear her streams repine."
→ FROM 'MARMION' BY Sir Walter Scott

CRAIGMILLAR CASTLE, EDINBURGH.

NB IN CURTAIN WALL NOTE OYSTER SHELL PINNINGS

No wonder Jon enjoyed this with its multiplicity of (barrel vaulted) chambers, & all those turnpike stairs, cavernous embrasures & dungeons. From the topmost terrace roof we looked down into a honeycomb of compartments, & across to Arthur's Seat & Pentland Hills. I sat & sunned in cosy corners this January day thinking of Mary Queen of Scots so often here. Those two ancient sentinel yews impressed me, the history, & the C14 Preston coat of arms.

Jon says: " So far, the best things about Scotland:- climbing Scott Monument, & scrambling on Arthur's Seat; & my favourite Castle is Dirleton second is Craigmillar, finding dungeons & climbing parapets."

"This castle hath a pleasant seat; the air, Nimbly & sweetly recommends itself Unto our gentle senses" MACBETH. W.Sh.

But oh! a windy day is no day for exposed castles; draughts whistle down passages, blasts scalp you on ramparts, gusts tear at note books & bite fingers & toes, UGH! On a still sunny winter day sheltered corners are blissful & picnic worthy. January 1985.

MORE CASTLES, & SCENIC SPLENDOUR.

Jon, having launched me, was unexpectedly packed off back to N.Zealand. Nevertheless, I continued to pursue this new interest he'd prompted.

Plying between Haddington & our Loch Alsh cottage, we would branch off the well kent route, taking in castles to E. & W. In fact we began to collect castles.

STIRLING CASTLE

BE SURE TO CLIMB THE OTHER GRANDSTAND, THE WALLACE MONUMENT

presides on its rocky commanding escarpment as a milestone seen from afar. He who stands on Edinburgh's ramparts must also climb Stirling's. 1984 One roasting hot July day, too thankful for a shady climb, I took the tree-clad cliff walk, only Douglas Garden as in a crow's nest, & cooled off on the parapet walk of to a grand landscape, looking beyond Wallace Mont with the Perthshire peaks, Ben Vorlich, & Ochils, etc.

"Look! Castle Stalker! Most imperative to sketch here."

"Stop! Invergarry Castle will enhance a picnic!"

"Hi! Kildrummy Castle! A batch of sketches here, so coffee break requir'd"

FINGERS NIPY NIPY COLD
JAN 10 1985
(15)

BLACKNESS CASTLE FIRTH OF FORTH
Some fort! Gun loops all round, fine keep, see snowy Ochils from parapets. Sailing boats. Don't miss, JUST THE PLACE FOR YOUNGSTERS

Many western castles perch'd on rock outcrops fill their sites to the limit with scenic splendour

HUNTLY CASTLE ABERDEEN
CARVED DETAILS MUCH WEATHERED (12·9·79)
1602

ARROW SLITS & DEEPLY SPLAYED GUN LOOP, BLACKNESS

"WHAT DO YOU FIND TO ENGAGE YOU SO MUCH IN THESE CASTLE RUINS? WHAT DO YOU LOOK FOR?" ASKED AN INCREDULOUS SASSENACH.

JUNE 1977

BREACHACHA CASTLE, ISLAND OF COLL.
What a spot! Right away on the Island's tip. Yet, 1773 Dr Johnson & Boswell reach'd here! Isolated? Yes! How Jon would love these rocks on cockle beach. DETAILS IN "HIGHLAND DAYS" BY D·A·G

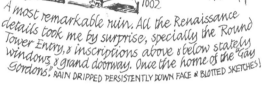

A most remarkable ruin. All the Renaissance details took me by surprise, specially the Round Tower Entry, & inscriptions above & below stately windows, & grand doorway. Once the home of the "Gay Gordons". RAIN DRIPPED PERSISTENTLY DOWN FACE & BLOTTED SKETCHES!

KISIMUL CASTLE (15)

CASTLE BAY, BARRA.
MacNeil stronghold. "MACNEIL HAS DINED, KINGS, & PRINCES MAY NOW DINE." Sailing by, May'67 we both recalled Bourtzi Castle in Nauplia Bay. SEE DETAILS OF BARRA IN DAYS IN W.HIGHLANDS BY DA

I LOOK FOR:-
Fortress qualities, Masonry, stones, Protruding rock, Mason's marks.

BARMKINS

I ENJOY:-
Wall walks, roof top views, turnpike stairs, barrel vaults, nooks, seated embrasures.

OVERSAILS

CASTLE TIORAM (13)
Macdonald stronghold astonishing sight in Loch Moidart, cut off at high tide. We paddled across at low tide to get the feel & atmosphere.

(15) CASTLE KENNEDY
17·4·77
We drove from Stranraer to see the famed Lochinch Gardens laid out by the Earl of Stair [George II 1740] having already visited Logan House Garden with its rich exuberance of rare plants. What a climate this is for growth! The tall ivy clad ruined stronghold, burnt 1715, lies between Black & White Lochs.
MOST PICTURESQUE RHODOS OUT!

MUNESS CASTLE UNST (16)
While in Shetland we had to see this most northerly of all castles in Britain [ALSO SAW MOST NORTHERLY POST OFFICE IN THICK MIST.] 2·6·70

I NOTICE:-
Putlog holes, brackets, weep holes, corbelling, sentry turrets, flues, hatches, splays.

JAMBS

I DRAW:-
Towers, bartizans, reads, machicolations, plans, bastions, gun loops, arrow slits, parapets, merlons, decorative carvings, heraldry etc

I READ:-
Histories, Records, Captivating stories, etc

CORNICES

DUNNOTTAR CASTLE (14)
I walked pleasantly the 2 mls S of Stonehaven climbed up on to this rock headland. What a history here! Scottish Regalia, Whigs, Covenanters etc & magnificent scenery. 2·9·83

DOUNE CASTLE (14)
on a bluff between rivers Teith & Ardoch. Glorious spot. Don't miss it. Our breakfast picnic was a joy! 20·7·75
Queens were here. Huge wide fireplace. Wall walks. How can one represent such a monster fort on this tiny scale? Morning country smells -- lovely!!
TWO OLD BRIDGES TO MUSE ON.

PLANS
SWEE COE KIT RO N

Keeps, curtain walls, & plans, often restricted by available rock space. All tell a tale.

SOUND OF MULL
DUART (13) CASTLE (MACLEAN)
stands in grand silhouette gracing the superb island mountain landscape. ON OUR ISLAND SAILS, WE ALWAY HAILED THIS FOCAL PT.

(16) LOCH RANZA CASTLE
ARRAN. [Did Bruce land at this spot?] We regaled here. Across the Sound lies Skipness (13 castle.

(13 EILEAN DONAN CASTLE, LOCHALSH, once seat of the Macraes lay on our route to the cottage. Our neighbour Macrae was once its keeper. ROMANTICALLY PICTURESQUE.

STIRLING

Approaching from N. in January (a day of sparkling hard white frost) there, ahead, hung, in the dim blue heavens, a visionary fairy palace, THE CASTLE, floating high above a shawl of mist. If this had been my first visit to STIRLING, no better nor more romantic introduction could have been devised.

CASTLE & PALACE

What ample lavish sleeves!

Flatulence.

External carvings seen against sun or in deep shadow.

Its dominating position, its 3 fortified gateways, its batteries, its towers, Parliament Hall, Chapel Royal, gardens, parapet views, Kings Own Building, squares, — as well as all this, are those sculptured enrichments of the Renaissance Palace. Who would not be struck by these delights among otherwise austere buildings?

So original so vital so bulgy full blown

enterprising sculptors.

Who is this? James V?

All much weathered.

No room to draw woman with cat on her shoulder.

A friendly & helpful Custodian this January day.

Use binocs to inspect this curious assortment of characters & their bottle legs!

Inside the Palace are the Stirling Heads, [carved oak roundels,] which once enriched the Presence Chamber.

2 of the Stirling Heads

SEE ALSO THE GREAT HALL (NOW BEING RESTORED) WHERE THAT SUMPTUOUS, FANTASTIC, BAPTISMAL BANQUET WAS HELD 1594

Below the Castle is a nucleus of this famous Royal Burgh's historic buildings: Mars Wark, Argyll Lugeing (now Youth Hostel,) the Guildhall, Church of the Holy Rude, & in Broad St, The Tolbooth, Market Cross, prosperous merchants' houses & Darnley's Hse.

A nest of pinnacles like flames

THE WALLACE MONUMENT Another landmark & steep climb up Abbey Craig. WHAT A VIEW OF BENS & PEAKS! NOT A SOUL DID I SEE THERE THIS JANUARY DAY. 1985

ORIGINAL UNICORN OF MARKET CROSS

THE FOUR FACED CLOCK TOWER OF TOLBOOTH with pavilion roof & gilded weathercock, SIR W. BRUCE 1704.

THE BUTTRESSED CHOIR, CHURCH OF THE HOLY RUDE This 5 sided Apse, rising ahead as you mount the hill, really is a knockout sight. J KNOX '59 preached when JAMES VI crowned here '67 SEE THE OPEN TIMBER ROOF.

BELL TOWER

INITIALLED TWIN LAMPS AT ENTRANCE GUILDHALL

JOHN COWANE

IN HIS NICHE

Now the GUILDHALL, this Hospital was erected by John Cowane, Dean of Guild, for the entertainment of "decayed Gild Brether 1639."

How fortunate for me, that Anna S & Pat A & I have made acquaintance

NO ROOM ON THIS PAGE TO INCLUDE WHAT MOST MOVED ME IN STIRLING — THE 4 ARCHED ANCIENT, HISTORIC, BRIDGE ACROSS THE FORTH. AS I DREW, PRAMS WERE RATTLING OVER THE COBBLES, FLOOD WATER SWISHING BELOW. IT IS SAID, NINE MONARCHS OF OLD CROSSED BY THESE MEDIEVAL PARAPETS.
See page 15

LENNOXLOVE, IN THE FERTILE E·LOTHIAN LANDSCAPE

THE SUPERB TREES OF ITS S·FACING SLOPES & POLITICIANS' WALK, MAKE MAGICAL VISITS IN FLOWERY SPRING & AUTUMN.

"When we build let us think that we build for ever"
said John Ruskin 1860

"The house of everyone is to him as his castle and fortress"
said Edward Cole 1590

Silver Casket, filigree, burnted, from Dauphin to Mary Q of Scots. This held those incriminating letters between herself and Bothwell.

AS A ONE TIME SCULPTOR THIS FIGURE AMUSED ME! 1679

OCTAGONAL SUNDIAL CARYATID. A SMILING LADY HOLDING ROSE & DRAPERIES. TWO BOWS BEHIND

So fascinated was I by the story of this curious title that, During my first holiday visit to Haddington from London in 1954, the priority expedition was to Lennoxlove, home of the Duke of Hamilton. We cycled, but could of course have walked. Approaching, my eye, not yet tuned in to tower houses, reacted with surprise to the fortress like appearance, until it travelled up thro' lofty trees to the cap house perched on top of the later C17+ mansion beyond. An endearing sight was the silvery star, spread wide across the lawn, thick with glistening snowdrops.

ONE HERD OF ONLY 2 EXTANT
WHITE CADZOW CATTLE

Inside this C14 Lethington Tower, the massive dimensions & stones of the vaulted Hall held me in thrall. I peopled it with influential figures of earlier centuries, to times when smoke from a central blazing fire would issue through roof outlets.

THROUGH THE HAMILTON CREST

PETIT POINT 1650

The death mask of Mary Q· of Scots; the silver casket given her by the Dauphin; Gray's Poems [designs by William Blake;] arms of the fireplace screen with coronet & initials of the Duchess of LENNOX; la Belle Stewart; these were of special interest to me also of course the fine & distinctive collections gathered here.

IN THE PETIT POINT ROOM, SEEK THESE 1650 COUNTRYSIDE STITCHED MOTIFS SEWN ON TO THE WOVEN WALL COVERING

"What would the world be once bereft Of wet & of wildness? Let them be left". wrote G.M. Hopkins.

Good walking here among the sequestered hills of the Lammermuirs, & memorable dips in the soft water of moorland burns. Lots to explore:– the Hopes & Whiteadder Reservoirs, the villages, each of distinctive character:– Gifford, Garvald, Stenton, Spott, FARMS! E·Linton, Morham, Oldhamstocks, Innerwick, – see "EAST LOTHIAN" by D·A·G· 1980 – also skylines:– Deuchrie, Tollis Hill, Monynut, Spartleton, Twin Law, Lammer, Priest Law, Killpallet, we walked them all, & more.

GLAMIS CASTLE

Glimpsing at last these glamorous turrets beyond shimmering leafy trees gave me a thrill, & the stately approach between James VI & Charles I, high on their plinths lent a special spice to this pregnant moment.

The small door of entry was to me a trifle disappointing tho' not of course surprising & well in keeping.

Once inside, the barrel vault, thick deep walls, & curved window soffits of the crypt, pricked my imagination.

The Queen Mother's close association with these ancient stones makes this gracious seat extra special & we were allowed to see both her bed & sitting apartments, very much in character. PLASTER WORK CEILINGS, FURNITURE, PORTRAITS, ETC, ALL HISTORIC. NOTICE GRATING IN HOLLOW NEWEL OF WHEEL STAIRS. EARLY CENTRAL HEATING!

I lingered on the roof. Views across the Vale of Strathmore, the Sidlaws, the Grampians; the richness of trees below; the lacey parapet railings; the turrets & their topknots seen at close range from above [I had to draw them]; all these combined to make a theatrical experience.

CLOCK TOWER FACING CENTRAL MAIN AVENUE

I WAS SO CLOSE AS TO BE ALMOST IN CONTACT WITH THE SLATER OF THIS PINNACLE

KING CHARLES I

KING JAMES VI

BAROQUE SUNDIAL 1680 A GLOBE OF MANY FACETS 21' TALL 84 DIALS

MOTIFS FROM ROOF RAILING

ST·ANDREW'S TOWER OF REFUGE G·ESK 1826 ON THE MODLACH.

THE QUEEN'S WELL Q·VICTORIA DRANK HERE 1861·G·ESK 6 FLYING BUTTRESSES

THE GLENS OF ANGUS, CLOVA, PROSEN, ESK, & SO ON, ARE BEAUTIFUL & VERY GOOD WALKING.

IN GLEN PROSEN FOUNTAIN BOWL WILSON·SCOTT· STH·POLE 1912

AIRLIE MONUMENT BOER WAR 1902 G·PROSEN, G·CLOVA

Our Haddington neighbour P.L., in 1966 introduced me to this delightful countryside from her cottage at DYKENEUK, Tarfside, Glen Esk.

In 1979 we joined Edinburgh University Extra Mural Tour to Castles of Aberdeenshire, & contended with 4 days of richly concentrated diet which required much sorting on our return. Our enthusiasm infected Emilia, who wrote with her modern turn of phrase :- "I'm sold on turrets." So we made <u>Tower Houses</u> our speciality when she & Renzo next visited us from Italy.

CRAIGIEVAR (1620) CASTLE

Can it be real? Am I dreaming? This compact fairy-tale-like fantasy in such stylish taste, rises neatly from its site with curved corners, & in confident assurance to end with a flourish of skyline conical turrets, ogee domes, dormers, chimneys, parapets, gables, spouts, in a romantic explosion, spirited & exuberant. Oh joy,

DOE NOT WAIKEN
SLEEPING DOGS

how it kindled me & enthused E! Continuously occupied since birth, it is richly embellished inside:- moulded plaster ceilings; groined Renaissance Hall vault; timber screens; musicians gallery; lettered fireplace motto; & views, yes, VIEWS — for its high situation [between Alford & Lumphanan] gives outlooks across to the valley of Don. THANK YOU, N.TRUST.

CLAYPOTTS CASTLE 1569

Most curious to see a cluster of crows nests, [2 in fact!] perched upon 2 drum towers! at opposite corners of the block, & 2 separate stair turrets. It bristles with gunloops. I longed to explore inside, but CLOSED. Au revoir! Must call again.

CRATHES CASTLE 1596

I FEARED my memory might [1958] confuse Crathes & Craigevar. BUT, NO. The painted ceilings, the impressive stone walls of Tower Room; the jewelled Hunting Horn of Leys; the Alexander Burnett chair; the arched window bays, & above all the garden, ensure the separate identity of this baronial seat. Have you ever seen such yew hedges? such a riot of flowers? such a magic carpet of colour? such expertise in gardening? BRAVO N·T.

My companion, also a BURNETT & also a garden lover & gardener, brings all her friends to visit here, 1958.

CRATHES

MUSICIANS FROM CHAMBER OF MUSES, painted Ceiling well worth the neckache!

AMISFIELD TOWER 5 m/s N OF DUMFRIES

C16

Another 'fairy tale' tower, quite remarkable. A 'doocot' of apartments suspended on the parent tower. [Don't forget the shopping list!]

I went to see the hand-carved door Samson & Lion, in fine state of preserve, boldly carved in oak. Similar job can be seen in TRAQUAIR

NOW IN MUSEUM OF ANTIQUITIES EDINBURGH

ONE CAN SCARCELY BEAR TO OMIT:- EDZELL, ELCHO, AIRLIE, ASCREAVIE, FYVIE, MIDMAR, MENZIES, CAELAVEROCK, FRASER, TOLQUHON, & OTHERS OF GREAT INTEREST. IN KINROSS-SHIRE EACH OF THE MANY CASTLES IS SAID TO BE IN SIGHT OF AT LEAST ONE OTHER FOR BEACON WARNING OF APPROACHING ENEMIES.

THESE, APART FROM MANY OTHER MEMENTOES, INSIST ON BEING INCLUDED:-

GLASGOW'S ⊕ BURRELL COLLECTION IS REWARDING, AGAIN & AGAIN

FROM TAPESTRY ALTAR FRONTAL

JEREMIAH STAINED GLASS

COMMANDO MEMORIAL
AT THE JUNCTION OF 3 HIGHLAND ROADS. COUNTLESS TIMES WE PASSED THIS ON OUR WAY TO THE BALMACARA COTTAGE, L'ALSH.

DUNDEE MUS.
INVERNESS MUS.
MUCH REDUCED OF COURSE
MEIGLE MUSEUM.
ANIMAL FORMS INCISED ON PICTISH STONES IN VARIOUS MUSEUMS.

MEMORABLE MOMENT.
SHAGGY BEASTS OUTLANDISH, BUT QUITE DOCILE. TYPICAL HIGHLAND CATTLE. GLAMOU! THEIR SETTING WITH TAWNY GOLDEN COATS. 3 SUDDENLY APPEARED IN OUR TRACK

I WAS AMUSED TO MEET THIS FELLOW CARVED, HALF HIDDEN UNDER A SOFFIT. ELGIN CATHEDRAL

FROM CAMEL CARAVAN ON TAPESTRY RUG. BRODIE CASTLE

"Whence springs the power of Scottish grit
Staunch loyalty bold enterprise;
Her grand romance of wizard wit
Whence did these glorious gifts arise?

The hardy sons of Scotia's soil
Their steadfast will and dauntless courage
Their martial and their mental toil
Were supped from the bowl of oatmeal porridge!"

TATTIE BOGLE SCARE CROW

A MOUTHIE HELPS THE "MILES ALONG; A STOUT HEART TAE A STEY BRAE"

FLORA MACDONALD'S DOG. SCULPTURE. INVERNESS

TWIN BEARS GUARD HIGH GATES. TRAQUAIR HSE.

DOO COT LECTERN TYPE
WITH S. FACING ROOF NESTS FOR 1,000 PIGEONS. MANY SUCH IN E. SCOTLAND

PERTH 1747
SCHOONER
CLEARLY DEPICTED IN RELIEF ON TOP ½ OF TOMBSTONE, ANCIENT CHURCHYARD.

WOOD & IVORY
CHESS PAWNS BURNS HSE. MUSEUM DUMFRIES

WHISKY DISTILLERIES
M. & I. FOLLOWED THE WHISKY TRAIL 1977 VIA TOMINTOUL, DUFFTOWN, KEITH, ETC. bought many bijou samples

RESTORED HEBRIDEAN CROFTER'S BLACK HOUSE, THATCHED.

FIDELIS IN ADVERSIS

I SAW THIS MORTSAFE AT CHANNELKIRK, OVER A GRAVE, AGAINST BODY-SNATCHING

PERTH
KINNOULL HILL CLIFF TOP.
ANOTHER FOLLY WITH SUPERB VIEW OF R. TAY & HILLS. DO CLIMB UP.

OBAN
McCAIG ROUND TOWER MEMORIAL
"THIS "COLOSSEUM" FOLLY (GRANITE) WITH SPECTACULAR VIEW OF SEAS, ISLANDS, MOUNTAINS, IS WELL WORTH THE CLIMB TO A SEAT (S)

THE PINEAPPLE GARDEN RETREAT
DUNMORE PARK. AIRTH
I was enchanted when, after years of 'itch' I ran to earth this imaginative & whimsical gem, & examined the coursed & cantilevered masonry with interest. Thro' the arch below, a columned portico leads on to S. lawn.

PRESTON MILL R. TYNE E. LINTON
'PICTURESQUE' IS THE WORD FOR THIS. RED PANTILED POLYGONAL ROOF, WITH VENTILATOR. ALL IN WORKING ORDER

NORRIE

INVERARY ON LOCH FYNE
black & white
31.8.85.
This alluring village, purpose built 1760-; holds me in thrall. I also drew smaller scenes in spite of a pushing, pulling, blustering wind;- Fisher Row, Ark Land, Crombies Place.

THE TAY, AT ABERFELDY.
IMPRESSIVE ROW OF POPLARS HERE
This imposing Wade Bridge, designed by Wm Adam 1733, has unique distinction & will always remain clearly etched in my memory. Black Watch Mon.t overlooks it.

⊕ See also in further books listed on back cover.

ISLANDS, ISLANDS, & MORE ISLANDS.

CANNA, RHUM, CUILLINS, EIGG, ARDNAMURCHAN PT
ALL SEEN WITH EXCITEMENT AS WE ROUNDED MULL FROM TOBERMORY.

SKYE THE WINGED ISLE
MULL THE BABE
ARRAN THE KIDNEY
ISLAY THE BOW

What is it that makes thoughts of an island
so attractive? How many are there off the W.
coasts? Names roll readily off the tongue,
so very many, that one is tempted to list an ISLAND
ALPHABET:—

Arran, Barra,
Benbecula,
Bute, Coll,
Colonsay,
Canna,
Cumbrae,
Dutchman's Cap,
Eriskay,
Eigg,
Fuday,
Fladda,
GARVELLACHS,
Gigha,
Gometra,
Handa,
Harris,
Islay,
Iona,
Jura,
Kerrera,
Lewis,
Lismore,
Lunga,
Muck,
Mull,
Noss, Papa
Westray,
Raasay,
Rhum,
Seil,
Skye,
Shiants,
Soay,
Staffa,
Stroma,
Tiree,
Tanera,
Treshnish,
Uist,
Ulva,
Unst,
Watersay,
Whalsay,
Yell

PUFFINS, QUAINT, CURIOUS LITTLE ODDITIES

SHAGS

GANNETS

KITTIWAKES

GUILLEMOTS

SOUND OF MULL.

'THE CALEDONIAN' PASSES LISMORE LIGHTHOUSE & DUART CASTLE

Mac Brayne's Ferry, eager with passengers, makes its sunlit way
from Oban to Tobermory & rounds the headland of Mull.
At once, up come the binoculars. Yes, away & ahead
the great bulk of Rhum, the cliffs of Canna & the spurr
of Eigg. Cuillin peaks too. Singular profiles all.
Now the Treshnish 'flotilla' to S, Dutchman's Cap
distinctive, those brooding Bens of Mull, & the 3
queenly Paps of Jura, all well loved contours to keen
island hoppers. EQUALLY WELL LOVED IS RAASAY'S CHIMNEY CONTOUR, & SPIKY SHIANTS
BOTH FARTHER NORTH.

CAIRN MORE C BEG FLADDA LUNGA DUTCHMAN'S CAP

MULL, & THE CHAIN OF THE TRESHNISH ISLES; STAFFA JUST OVER OUR HORIZON.

HOW A REALLY SMALL ISLAND CAN CAPTIVATE & CHARM!
We mount Iona's Dun I & gaze over jade
seas & silver sands in all directions.

We climb Tiree's Ben Hynish for a wide
spectacle of field patchwork & wide sweeping
bays, flowery headlands, & Skerryvore lighthouse.

CHOPPY SEA
TO GIGHA, BUT
HEAVENLY ONCE WE
ARRIVED
1972

We wander or cycle Gigha's length & find with joy
that east & west seas almost meet at the waist,
but fail to cut this dear green island into two.

We "beat the bounds" of Coll on small wheel hired
bicycles. Up & down we go though winds may tease.

AND ON ALL THESE HEADY & JOYFUL OCCASIONS I THINK:—

"I could skip out of my skin like a subtile snake
I feel so limber."

ON COLL
1972
DETAILS IN "DAYS IN
WEST HIGHLANDS, & ISLANDS"

ISLANDS CONTD

How stimulating was that low tide wade across from Colonsay over to Oransay, there to ponder, & contemplate the life of monks who carved those figured tomb slabs & built cloisters with pointed arches.

How "local & neighbourly" to take the short crossing from the remote ramparts of Jura, & ferry the narrow Sound, spotting skeins of geese, their sights set on those attractive grazing pastures.

How good to:-

sniff Benbecula's machair;	spot Fetlar's snowy owl;
find wheel houses on S. Uist;	visit Orkney's chambered cairn etc;
dance on Barra's coral strand;	explore the fastnesses of Rhum;
see Jura's stags so close at hand;	gasp at the Cuillin peaks on Skye;
climb Arran's Goat Fell etc;	perform a jig on Raasay's Dun Caan!

These are a few of the ISLANDS' gifts to me in May, June, September months, with the blessing of fine weather. I wanted to stretch each telling moment, each illuminating hour, & must treasure these days of renewal, their magic & hypnotic enchantment.

Jon. Wills, Rector Edinburgh Univ. 1970 rowed us over to Noss.

Oh, the times we had! Jotted eulogies, paeans of praise, jolly line sketches are all evocative of joy. So we relive these times with undying affection. I went from each visit as the Queen of Sheba from Solomon, starry eyed and loaded with treasures. ✳

BIRD WATCHER BOBBY TULLOCH gave up his passage on the overcrowded launch, unst to Yell.

on Rhum

"But grant me still a friend in my retreat
Whom I may whisper 'Solitude is sweet'"
W. COWPER

✧   ✧   ✧

My friend Betty P, was moved to write thus:-

KITTIWAKES

There's briar for a nosegay
And bracken for a bed,
And white heather flowering
Beneath our tread.

Softly the west wind murmurs
With sea born lullaby,
Till drowsed with sleep we cannot hear
The curlew's rippling cry.

GUILLEMOTS

An amber burn to drink our health,
Ripe bilberries to eat,
And yellow stonecrop twined with moss
A carpet for our feet.

A turquoise sea caresses
A bay of faded rose;
But will its whispers reach us?
Only the west wind knows.

PUFFINS

ASSEMBLY OF PREENING SHAGS
✳ More about ISLANDS in "Days in W. Highlands & Islands"

SOME THOUGHTS ABOUT WALKING

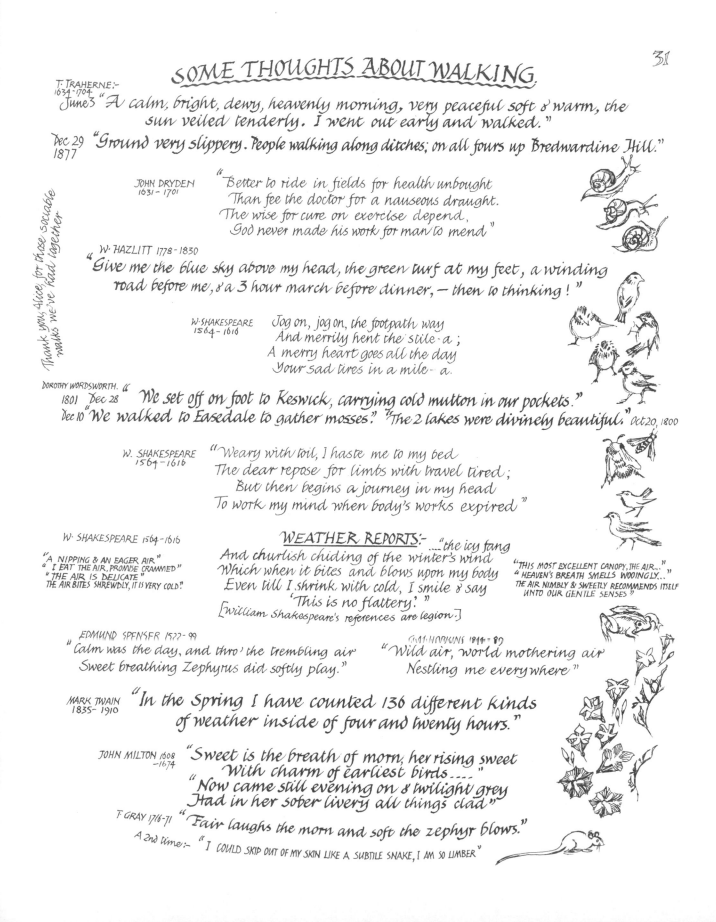

T. TRAHERNE:-
1634-1704

June 3 "A calm, bright, dewy, heavenly morning, very peaceful soft & warm, the sun veiled tenderly. I went out early and walked."

Dec 29 "Ground very slippery. People walking along ditches; on all fours up Bredwardine Hill."
1877

JOHN DRYDEN
1631-1701
"Better to ride in fields for health unbought
Than fee the doctor for a nauseous draught.
The wise for cure on exercise depend,
God never made his work for man to mend"

W. HAZLITT 1778-1830
"Give me the blue sky above my head, the green turf at my feet, a winding road before me, & a 3 hour march before dinner, — then to thinking!"

W. SHAKESPEARE
1564-1616
Jog on, jog on, the footpath way
And merrily hent the stile-a;
A merry heart goes all the day
Your sad tires in a mile-a.

DOROTHY WORDSWORTH. "
1801 Dec 28 "We set off on foot to Keswick, carrying cold mutton in our pockets."
Dec 10 "We walked to Easedale to gather mosses." "The 2 lakes were divinely beautiful." Oct 20, 1800

W. SHAKESPEARE
1564-1616
"Weary with toil, I haste me to my bed
The dear repose for limbs with travel tired;
But then begins a journey in my head
To work my mind when body's works expired"

WEATHER REPORTS:- ...the icy fang

W. SHAKESPEARE 1564-1616

"A NIPPING & AN EAGER AIR"
"I EAT THE AIR, PROMISE CRAMMED"
"THE AIR IS DELICATE"
THE AIR BITES SHREWDLY, IT IS VERY COLD."

And churlish chiding of the winter's wind
Which when it bites and blows upon my body
Even till I shrink with cold, I smile & say
'This is no flattery'."
[William Shakespeare's references are legion.]

"THIS MOST EXCELLENT CANOPY, THE AIR..."
"HEAVEN'S BREATH SMELLS WOOINGLY..."
THE AIR NIMBLY & SWEETLY RECOMMENDS ITSELF
UNTO OUR GENTLE SENSES"

EDMUND SPENSER 1522-99
"Calm was the day, and thro' the trembling air
Sweet breathing Zephyrus did softly play."

G.M. HOPKINS 1844-89
"Wild air, world mothering air
Nestling me everywhere"

MARK TWAIN
1835-1910
"In the Spring I have counted 136 different kinds of weather inside of four and twenty hours."

JOHN MILTON 1608
-1674
"Sweet is the breath of morn, her rising sweet
With charm of earliest birds....."
"Now came still evening on & twilight grey
Had in her sober livery all things clad"

T. GRAY 1716-71 "Fair laughs the morn and soft the zephyr blows."

A 2nd time:- "I COULD SKIP OUT OF MY SKIN LIKE A SUBTLE SNAKE, I AM SO LIMBER"

Thank you, Alice, for those sociable walks we've had together

" If music and sweet poetry agree
As they must needs [the sister & the brother]
Then must the love be great twixt thee & me
Because thou lov'st the one & I the other."
R. BARNFIELD 1574-1627

BY CHANCE.

Connie Fraser & I, both from S·LONDON crossed paths in an Edinburgh bookshop by the merest chance, after a blank gap of 60+years; LUCK INDEED! so our tenuous childhood frien'ship became pleasantly renewed & happily deepened.

Over a sherry one day she mused :-"You've had 20 years of retirement in Scotland & have drawn & written of its pleasures. Have you forgotten the England of your birth? If I fire at you the words "English Villages" which leap to your mind? or the word 'Countrysides' is there one above all others for you?" She paused a moment, then ventured, "I know the word 'CATHEDRALS' would produce an avalanche of outpourings, & 'CHILDHOOD' is best reserved until some future date."

Such promptings set my mind working at high speed, scudding thro' village, town, city, countrysides; thro' museums, galleries, churches, cathedrals; round coasts, & across the wide tapestry of places, persons, associates, & friends which the crammed & fruitful years inevitably bring.

Sketch books full of drawings, some at hand, some unearthed, spurred me on. But many, sadly, had perished in the London blitz, others by ruthless carefree burnings, or during various house removals. I determined however to set down in due course some memories for C·F· to mull over. Trifles they may be, trivial some are; but "little things are infinitely more important" said CONAN DOYLE

"Look, what thy memory cannot contain
Commit to these waste blanks & thou shalt find
Those children nursed, delivered from thy brain
To take a new acquaintance of thy mind.
These offices, so oft as thou wilt look,
Shall profit thee, & much enrich thy book." W·SH

HERE & THERE IN ENGLAND

A Record of Joy.

Recalling visits & reviving incidents from "thumbnail" sketches, inevitably brings memories woven inextricably with friends & friendly faces.

"Ah! heavenly joy! But who hath ever heard,
Who hath seen joy, or who shall ever find
Joy's language? There is neither speech nor word;
Nought but itself to teach it to mankind." R BRIDGES

Then Maida (EX-PATRIOT SCOT NOW IN OXFORD, & WHOSE PEN SPILLS VERSE,) asked, "What about London, your birthplace, & England? Surely they could have some jottings! Playfully she wrote a D.A.GOODCHILD acrostic after my books on Scotland appeared. TWO OF THE 17 LINES :–

"Doris, don't stop! Recast your spell,
Conjure more magic from your well..."

But where should I begin on what must be a highly selective project?

"Just start", I urged myself, "& see what happens. Nothing comes of nothing! He who hesitates is lost!"

"Select the radiant peak moments, the highlighted images, small incidents, & cull from all these sketch books lying here close at hand."

"That is best which lieth nearest Shape from that thy work of art" H.W.L

But how to collate this collection of sporadic drawings done haphazardly in 30 odd note books, [spontaneous jottings, momentous, & swiftly depicted for the pure love of identifying with objects of visual pleasure;] do I present them in Regions, or Types, or freely as shape & space permits?

"I STAND IN PAUSE WHERE I SHALL FIRST BEGIN" HAMLET. W.Sh.

These are the problems of the amateur, but the compulsive urge to so record must be satisfied, & the "mystic chords of memory" secured while yet fresh.

'TODAY'S PLEASURES ARE TOMORROW'S TREASURES"

LONDON'S GRYPHON

LONDON BOBBIES EVER HELPFUL,

LONDON PIGEONS EVER HUNGRY. IN MOST LONDON SQUARES THEY HAVE SHARED MY PICNICS.

REMINDS ME OF THE MOSCOW METRO

MOG

VAULTED SUBWAY OF HIGH LEVEL R'LY STATION CRYSTAL PALACE OUR FAMILY LIVED NEAR AS DO ALISON & SOC NOW

After a gap of 70 yrs, Edna & Syd took me to see those monsters round the lake. NO WONDER AS A 10 YR OLD I FELL IN & NEARLY DROWNED! THAT ½ ML WALK HOME, SODDEN & DRIPPING, WAS NOT PLEASANT! WEEKLY SUMMER FIREWORKS SEEN FROM OUR TOP WINDOWS, & WINTER CONCERTS, ALL V GOOD.

GORILLA, D.WYNESS

THIS FLYING DRAGON, OF ST. MARY LE BOW, REMINDS ME OF ST BAVON CATH, GHENT.

I ALWAYS WINK UP AT THIS GRASSHOPPER WHEN NEAR THE ROYAL EXCHANGE & THINK OF SIR THOMAS GRESHAM

THE ROEBUCK

GREETINGS TO GRACE L, WESTMINSTER

CUTTY SARK

THE FAMOUS OLD CLIPPER, SHIPPED TEA FROM CHINA (19 NOW IN DRY DOCK GREENWICH NEAR FRANCIS CHICHESTER'S GIPSY MOTH. HERE I RECALL SUDDEN MEETING, PAT W- & GREENWICH PARK PICNICS

GRYPHON WIND VANE. I DID NOT ENJOY SMITHFIELD MKT BUT ST BARTHOLOMEW THE GREAT NEAR BY, WAS LIKE FINDING A PEARL IN A MIDDEN.

OUR INITIATION TO CAMPING, RENE S & I, WITH A.G. WAS IN WALTON-ON-THAMES IN PREPARATION FOR CAMPING TOUR IN SCOTLAND. 1928

CHINESE PAGODA KEW

IN A CANOPIED PUNT, MURIEL B & I TALKED & DOZED OUR TRANQUIL WAY DOWN RIVER BY DAY, WITH HILARIOUS FUN & GAIETY BY NIGHT ...THAMES 1927

WE SAW ONE HOUR ONLY OF HENLEY'S REGATTA [THOUGHTS OF MARGARET DAY] ON OUR WAY TO STIDNOR, TURVILLE & FINGEST, IN CHILTERNS. THAT TWIN GABLED NORMAN TOWER, & (& FONT, LID LOCKED AGAINST WATER STEALERS, MUCH INTERESTED US.

FINGEST CHURCH

JESTER MISERICORD

HENRY VII CHAPEL WESTMINSTER ABBEY

LACE LIKE GATES OF HAMPTON COURT, OUR MEETING PLACE AFTER BOATING UP THAMES

THAMES BOAT RACE

Hail, snowflakes boisterous wind, THESE WERE OUR FATE APRIL 1952 FOR A HUDDLED GLIMPSE OF BOAT RACE NEAR BARNES BRIDGE M.M.B P.F. DAG. ROBIN, TOM

OUTER RAMPARTS

TOWER OF LONDON, & GARDENS PICNIC. MOST ENJOYABLE BUT, BEST TO AVOID SUMMER SCHOOL HOLS & BANK HOLIDAYS, ENDLESS QUEUES FOR. POPULARITY OF RAVEN EXCEEDS CROWN JEWELS. POPULARITY OF RAVEN EXCEEDS EVEN THEM. I RECALLED BARNABY RUDGE.

ALBERT BRIDGE EXCITING SPECTACLE

1966 ONWARDS, I delighted in those fresh air picnic breakfasts by the Serpentine, Hyde Park after a night coach Edinburgh – London. A 2nd Mrs Mop shared my bench; "Its bein' sa cheerful as keeps me goin'"

LONDON, PERSONAL ENJOYMENTS.

1940

"Take immediate underground shelter if siren sounds, & remember how early tonight's blackout will be!" Thus cautioned, I set off pedal cycling in London 1940 Oct 27 to search out wall memorial plaques, inscriptions, epitaphs, & Epstein's Outdoor Sculptures. I was on a year's study course of stone carving & letter cutting. Daylight hours were very precious. After sunset nights were pitch black, in total darkness.

IRON RATION OF BREAD & PEA NUT BUTTER IN POCKET

These open air museums were new fields of study for me as I pedalled, starry eyed, from one work of art to the next, graveyard tombstones included.

During ensuing years the wide stone steps of the British Museum V.A Museum, Tate Gallery, Private, & National Galleries, have been well worn by my eager feet.

Inns of Court; Markets; have been loitered in; Historic Mansions, Halls, Parliament, visited; the R. Thames sailed; Concerts, Theatres have given full measure; Parks much enjoyed [breakfast to sunset;] writers, Evelyn, Pepys, Dickens & many another digested with pleasure. & how much more all these have to give! THERE IS NO END NO FULL STOP.

KARL MARX HIGHGATE CEMETERY. [I RECALL ANN S. & JILL P. WITH PLEASURE]

NIGHT   DAY
EPSTEIN SCULPTURES ON ST JAMES UNDERGROUND STN. [DRIZZLE FRUSTRATED, RAIN OBSTRUCTED - HAD TO GIVE UP!]

RIMA & BIRDS. STONE CARVED PANEL IN HYDE PARK 1924. MEMORIAL TO W.H. HUDSON. TARRED & FEATHERED, BUT NOT BY ME! IT INFLUENCED MY CARVING OF ST FRANCIS & BIRDS.

PROUD UPLIFTED HEAD OF MADONNA

FRYDERIK CHOPIN. TWO STH BANK SCULPTURES.

THE CELLIST BY
HAVING LOST MY TRAIN AT WATERLOO STN, I AMBLED ALONG, IN LEISURELY FASHION DISCOVERING PLAY PARK, SCULPTURES & SUCHLIKE AS WELL AS WATCHING RIVER CRAFT & VIEWS, RUNNERS, JOGGERS, BALLOONS, FANCY HATS ON MUSICIAN, BANNER MARCHERS, COLLECTING FOR CHARITIES, WITH ENORMOUS ENTHUSIASM, & GREAT JOLLITY.

PLAY PARK

MADAME SUGGIA, BY A. JOHN THE TATE GALLERY COLLECTION HOLDS WORKS OF WONDER WHICH AGAIN FILL ME WITH ECSTASY.

THESE TINY DRAWINGS ARE MEREST REMINDERS

VAN GOGH'S SUNFLOWERS

"MAN IN SCARLET TURBAN" J. VAN EYCK

WESTMINSTER ABBEY
"THE "JUDGEMENT OF SOLOMON" CARVED CAPITAL 1140. WHAT A SUBJECT! GO OFF SEASON FOR GOOD VIEWING.

3 FAVOURITE NATIONAL GALLERY PORTRAITS I GLOAT OVER THESE & MANY ANOTHER

"PORTRAIT OF A LADY" VAN DER WEYDEN

THE PINK BOW IS BEWITCHING "THE MUSIC MASTER" BY JAN STEEN AND I LIKE THE BLUE BOY CARRYING VIOL.

QUEEN BISHOP
FROM SET OF WALRUS TUSK CHESSMEN, LEWIS. FOR 50 YRS I'VE DOTED ON THESE CARVINGS

13 TARTAR LEADING A CAMEL P.G ON SILK.

THE BRITISH MUSEUM IS A TREASURE HOUSE OF ENTERTAINMENT.

WARRIORS IN COMBAT
530 BC
DECOR ON GREEK VASE

BOADICEA

THESE DIVERSE FEET, ALL IN SAME QUEUE ON SAME DAMP DAY, IN LINE FOR RENOIR EXHIBITION IN RAIN

GREETINGS TO ANN   EALING

WET? "A BIT" BORED? NO!
THESE KEEN TIRELESS FEET WILLING TO JOIN LONG QUEUE FOR A PEEP AT RENOIR PTGS 1985

PETRONIUS SAID:- "I have lived, nor shall maligner future Take from me what an earlier hour once gave"
A. HUXLEY TRANSLATION

Oh! that jolly picnic breakfast in the Barbican after a night's sleeper Edinb. to Kings X. Nov 30 My early rising seat companion had [by mischance] 2 new diaries. "I'll trade you one for a sketch" he proposed!

SOUTH EASTERLY

1940 "Take shelter at once if dog fights overhead & come back safely" we did. Eilidh & I were off on a Youth Hostel cycle tour of Surrey Sussex to see evacuated London friends, [a tour such as Edith & I took on foot in Kent, years before.] Those war years, parental concern was at high pitch for no pre planning could avoid the unpredictability of air raids & skirmishes.

Previously the PILGRIMS WAY along the N. Downs 1928 with Chaucer in my pocket, was my first long & momentous lone walk. Later, South Downland treks with Browning at hand, & days most romantic and exhilarating, endeared me to these alluring, softly rolling chalk hills fragrant with thyme, mint, fennel. THE ISLE OF WIGHT, its coasts & countryside held choice spots to be joyfully hunted out.

In recent years I have needed no scrap of persuasion from E & L to tour those folds of my beloved South Downs following a trail of tiny villages & little churches, primrose banks, violet hollows, & flowering dykes, open riverside footpaths, whaleback tracks, & woodland ways.

"Earth's crammed with heaven
And every common bush afire with God"
E.B.B.

& my sketch books are crammed with drawings as is this page! IT HAS TO BE SO!

FOOT TOWER! MARTELLO

CANTERBURY'S SOARING PINNACLES HERRINGBONE

ROMAN PHAROS LIGHTHSE DOVER 43 A.D.

SLATE SPIRE ROCHESTER CATHEDRAL V. MODEST

BODIAM CASTLE WATER LILY MOAT, BUT RAIN TODAY, UMBRELLAS ON THE PARAPETS

OAST HOUSES & BINES IN KENTISH HOP GARDENS.

FAMILIES IN DEPTFORD WHERE I WORKED, '29 to '34 WOULD MIGRATE, TO HAND PICK IN THE HOP FIELDS EACH JULY & AUGUST, LIVING LIKE GYPSIES, TO EARN A TRIFLE FOR NEEDED EXTRAS.

INTRINSIC BEAUTY

BATTLE ABBEY (B UNDERCROFT LOVELY TO SEE, DIFFICULT TO DRAW. A HAPPY VISIT TO THIS TOWN

HASTINGS NET SHOPS

SO SLACK, FUNCTIONAL, UNCOMMON, I HAD TO DRAW THEM.

NORMAN BARFRESTON CHURCH IN ITS TINY HAMLET WAS A BREATHLESS THRILL TO ME. [KILPECK, WINDRUSH, DALMENY,] I LONG FOR ANOTHER VISIT.

MOST ENGAGING

THE LONG WALLS, ANDERIDA ROMAN FORT, NORMAN CASTLE WITHIN & 1940 PILLBOXES

BRICK STONE FLINT RUBBLE

ROYAL PAVILION BRIGHTON A WHIMSICAL FANTASY APPROVED BY MY CHILDHOOD ROMANTICISM.

THE HUNCHBACK IN (4 CHANCEL OF DEMOLISHED CH WINCHELSEA-K) A CHARMING BACKWATER. STRAND GATE (13

A FEW SUSSEX VILLAGE CHURCH TOWERS & SPIRES

SOMPTING CH 4 GABLED SAXON TOWER; SHINGLED HELM ROOF;- RHENISH MY FIRST SAXON THRILL, 1927.

SOUTHEASE ROUND TOWER, CONICAL SPIRE, MEDIEVAL FRESCOES

RODMELL LEONARD & VIRGINIA WOOLF

PIDDINGHOE FLINT ROUND TOWER, SLATE COPPER STEEPLE, GILDED TROUT VANE, ON BLUFF ABOVE OUSE. A PLEASURE TO LINGER HERE.

WILMINGTON CH NEXT PRIORY

GREETINGS TO HELEN D

PEVENSEY CHURCH BLACKBIRD DIVERSION!

PHEASANT WEATHER VANE LEWES

LEWES AMMONITE CAPITAL OF GEOLOGIST'S HOUSE AVON WILDS. INDIVIDUALITY HERE, I LIKE IT!

WESTFIELD BUTTRESSES! 1542 IRON FIGURES ON OAK DOOR I HAVE A LIKING FOR BUTTRESSES

LILLINGSTONE 15 SQ TINY CHURCH, MASSIVE FLINT WALLS, BROACH BELFRY SPIRE, WEATHER BOARDED, LECTERN, FONT, ALTAR LOVELY!

FROM SEPULCHRAL SLAB

CARVED PIGEONS WEST DEAN

BISHOPSTONE

LONG MAN WILMINGTON

RYE IN MERMAID STREET UNIQUE I SAY THESE LIKE HENRY JAMES 2 DOOR KNOCKERS [DELIGHTFUL TOWN]

An invigorating switch back walk on springy turf along the edge of the 7 SISTERS chalk cliffs, is a good leg stretcher & lung expander!

BEACHY HEAD

SOUTH ENGLAND

Oast houses, broach spires, shingle roofs, thatched roofs; walls of silver grey flint & red brick, of stone, pebble, lath & plaster, of mathematical tiles, the whole gamut of varying surfaces have entertained & made claim. "dappled things; All things counter, original, spare, strange." — G.M.H.

Castles, Cathedrals, Great Manor Houses & Gardens, landscapes & many Weald towns have been well savoured. And the many friends of these parts; how well I remember them:-

NONIE B'S GENEROUS HOSPITALITY, IN FOLKESTONE, SHEILA McC's READY WELCOME, IN CHICHESTER, EDITH & L'S HOSPITABLE FELLOWSHIP, IN PEVENSEY, JOAN & AUDREY'S VISITED HOME, IN DORKING, JULIA & IAN'S CORDIAL INVITATIONS, IN ALTON, ALSO:-
SUE J; READY COLLABORATOR, IN LINDFIELD, PAMELA M; THE BOUNTIFUL, IN EASTBOURNE, ROSEMARY F; CALLIGRAPHER, IN MAIDSTONE, BARBARA B; TIE DYER, OF TUNBRIDGE WELLS, SANDRA M; ARTIST, ANIMAL LOVER, RAINHAM, JILL L; THE GENTLE LADY IN RUSTINGTON, MARIE A, DESIGNER; IN ALRESFORD, ELIZABETH F; STALWART PEN FRIEND, COBHAM, ERIK F; WALKER & LOVER OF POETRY, & MANY ANOTHER, HAVE ENRICHED THESE SCENES FOR ME, AS HAVE ALL THOSE YOUTH HOSTEL CONTACTS.

"Give to me the life I love, Let the lave go by me; Give the jolly heaven above And the byway nigh me." R.L.S

Echoes of past history visits to many Libraries with those enthusiasts EDITH & LAURENCE; thoughts of Churchill, readings of Dickens, Jane Austen, S Kaye Smith, H. Bellot, Chesterton, Tennyson, De la Mare, Kipling, & Mozart enthusiasts of Glyndebourne, THANK YOU ALL, & Thomas Hardy, for I find Wessex mementoes must appear on this page.

"Those friends thou hast and their adoption tried, Grapple them to thy heart with hoops of steel." W. Sh.

SOUTH WEST

When homeless from a flying buzz bomb of the London blitz — JUNE 1944
how welcome & relaxing it was to retreat to South Petherton &
find a homely Somerset welcome with Frank & Cicely,

"Soothed by every azure breath
That under heaven is blown." P.B.S

& to go exploring the countryside thereabout.

CHEDDAR GORGE & LIMESTONE CAVES Ca in December!

Ponies of New Forest, Dartmoor & Exmoor. [Lorna Doone associations. YES, WE SPOTTED THEM]

GLASTONBURY TOR had to be climbed [KING ARTHUR] AVALON

ABBOT'S KITCHEN MUSEUM & C.14 Abbot's Barn are sole remains of fine Abbey Buildings

CERNE ABBAS HILLSIDE GIANT HERCULES? Certainly a frightening fellow!

Years later hospitality from:-

Arthur & Marjorie NR AXMINSTER;
David & Jean in TRURO;
Marjorie W, PAIGNTON;
Eilidh K, TAUNTON;
Eve S, EXMOUTH;
& Betty T's presence in PLYMOUTH, gave me incentive to see for myself these south westerly parts.
Thomas Hardy's Wessex
Gilbert White's Selborne
Lorna Doone's Exmoor vale
were highlights, but,

NEAR LYNMOUTH 1929 From the old horse drawn caravan we all could nip down the cliff for a bathe or take a risky naked cold waterfall shower under the cliff [no one else thereabout] in this my introduction to Devon.

In 1950 I joined A&M at their campsite near Saltash; in 1955 joined H&A, Marion in their Perranporth bungalow; in 1964 joined D & J in their Malpas home [USEFUL BROTHERS & SISTERS I SAY!]

DUNSTER YARN MKT caught my eye at once with its 8 gables holding hands. Old houses; Mill; Priory Ch; Inn; C.12 Castle on hill. All delight.

CULBONE'S tiny church. We walked from PORLOCK WEIR 1942 with thoughts of Coleridge negotiating the wooded hillside of the combe.

REMEMBER ALABASTER FROM WATCHET. C.B.A CLIFF

"which of all the lovely scenes most held you?" was the question.

Wild daffs in the Umborne Valley;
Cyclamen at Killerton & Brixham;
Cathedrals of course;
Somerset's GOLDEN HAM HILL STONE Church Towers;
those fine carved wooden ... Screens, Devon;
the Tors of Dartmoor;
lunar landscape of china clay pyramids at St Austell;
clapper bridges,
HEPWORTH SCULPTURE, LEACH POTTERY,
& those entrancing fishing villages,
cliffs & coves as far as LAND'S END. There,

"I stood as on some mighty eagle's beak
Eastward the sea absorbing
Viewing nothing but sea & sky." W.W.H

WEST PENTIRE DIVING   SEA ANEMONES   HOUSEL BAY WITH G's & C's

NAT TRUST COTTAGES SELWORTHY We walked from MINEHEAD via Selworthy Beacon with delight

MAIN HALL C.14

1934 DARTINGTON HALL, its Trees & fellowship. Curiosity brought me here in W.B. Curry's time. Later it was CRAFT COURSES that claimed me, also the Music.

STADDLE STONES FOR HAY.

ST AUSTELL Catching sight of the shining white pyramids of China Clay took my breath 24 hrs ago. Today Barb. Hepworth's sculpture took my breath and Bernard Leach's Pottery delighted ST IVES 1947

ST MICHAEL'S MOUNT. LOW TIDE CAUSEWAY WALK V. PLEASANT. "WHAT A MUSTERING OF SAINTS IN CORNWALL!"

THE COSY CURVES OF THATCH— INSULATION NEVER USED ON W. EXPOSED ROOFS. WINDOWS PEEP OUT FROM UNDER BLANKET, VERY COSSETED!

JASMINE MUFFLED LATTICES

1934 Steerage passage London to Plymouth, then cycling home thro' southern counties gave me my first visit to:-

EXETER CATHEDRAL That continuous stone vault, nave to chancel; its bosses; the twin transept towers; the 12 carved minstrels with cymbals, timbrel, shawm, gittern, organ, trumpet, harp, viol, recorder, bagpipe, citole; carved corbels, Lady Chapel shepherds, all engrossing

1984 visit with Eve S & Marjorie W, specially good

TUMBLER & VIOLIST PERFORM BEFORE VIRGIN

POLPERRO, MEVAGISSEY HARBOUR, LOOE, FOWEY, COVERACK, ETC, ALL INVITING— IN [WINTER]

GORRAN HAVEN

LOBSTER POTS

St Mary's Cathedral

1952 MINACK THEATRE among granite cliffs, & above fine white PORTHCURNO beach SEE ALSO IN "DAYS IN THE W. HIGHLANDS & ISLANDS

D & J's garden looks down on to St Mary's Cathedral 1910. Assembly Rooms, Georgian Lemon St, Regency Terraces, Walsingham Cresc, all have presence here. Museum, special!

RESTING SPECTATOR — CORBEL

"Friendship redoubleth joys, & cutteth griefs in halves." FRANCIS BACON 1561-1626.

BRISTOL & AROUND

1941

When exhausted from the Bristol blitz 1941-8 tired with nights of dreary fire watching, how refreshing to cycle across the Avon Gorge Suspension Bridge, 8 miles away on deserted country roads exploring hills & vales. Fresh farm eggs were gold! You might win one or even two, from a friendly farmer OR BY CHANCE STUMBLE ON ONE IN THE FARMYARD!! A glass of real milk was a boon, rasps & straws in season, Victoria plums & pears, a prize.

SHEPTON MALLET MKT CROSS. NO ROOM FOR MORE MENDIP VILLAGES:- CHEDDAR, CHEW MAGNA, AXBRIDGE, DUNDRY BEACON.

Then as grist to the mill of craft, & to overcome depleted stocks & strict rationing of yarns etc, we went off wool gathering along fences, withy pulling from hedges, clay digging in ditches; chalk lifting from quarries, winkling alabaster from cliffs, gathering pine needles for straw work etc.*

WALKING NEAR BRISTOL & I, STUMBLED ACROSS WITH FIRE ON THE EDGE OF A COPSE, NATURE'S SCULPTURE! TWISTED TAP ROOT, 3 SURFACE ROOTS; A PHOENIX RISEN FROM THE ASHES, MY MASCOT. I LIVED A CHARMED LIFE TILL 1984 THE GARDENER CHOPPED IT FOR FIREWOOD! BAA HOO! 1945 SUE J, PEGGY M. A LARCH TREE BOLE, CHARRED A REMARKABLE ARBOREAL.

THE ELEGANT SPA CITY OF BATH a mere bus ride from Bristol, was a very popular diversion for us in the 1940's; Roman Baths; Pump Room; Tompion Clock 1709; Georgian city; picnics by Pulteney Bridge; the Cathedral & those angels negotiating the ladders of Jacob's dream; Bishop Oliver King's rebus, all have undying appeal. Don't you agree, Kate? Enjoyable visit today 1981 but sorry to miss you.
'ΑΡΙΣΤΟΝ ΜΕΝ ΥΔΩΡ' WATER IS BEST!'
[FROM BATH, SOON IN BRADFORD ON AVON, SO VERY PICTURESQUE, BUT NO ROOM HERE FOR MORE.]

OLIVE & CROWN

The Bristol Theatre Royal was the very summit of pleasure with Restoration Comedy Ballet Toos etc. Orchestral Concerts & bright pursuits fed our hunger for social & civilised living.

REFUGEES

WHAT A BONANZA OF CARVINGS FROM LUMPS OF CHALK & ALABASTER. CREATIVE LITTLE PAT. C. TURNED A STICK OF BLACKBOARD CHALK INTO A MADONNA; PINE NEEDLES BECAME DOLLS HATS; HEDGE ROWS GAVE BASKETS & TOAST RACKS; CLAY, COILED POTS, & ARMY SNOW COATS, PARACHUTES & TORN SHEETS WERE TRANSFORMED INTO STAGE COSTUME. KATE C. PHYLL H. DID LIKEWISE

MALMESBURY, WILTS, hill top town of such attraction we always call en route, Oxford to Bristol, 1950's to see the south porch Romanesque sculptures of the superb Abbey, the Manuscript, Market Cross etc & to picnic. June 1985

MKT CROSS

"Give me to fashion a thing *
Give me to make & to mould
I have found out the song I can sing
I am happy delivered & bold."

" I too will something make
And joy in the making,
Although tomorrow it seem
Like the empty words of a dream
Remembered on waking."
R. BRIDGES.

These were times when daylight gleanings made blackout pleasures. I also took piano lessons in the flat below, MOST CONVENIENTLY !
JULY 79, VISITED JANE & RICHARD BETWEEN TRAINS!

ST MARY REDCLIFFE

THIS PARISH CHURCH MIRACULOUSLY STANDING WHEN SO MANY BRISTOL 1940 CHURCHES BLITZED WAS AS A LIGHT IN THE DARKNESS BY ITS SINGULAR BEAUTY. (15 SPIRE; C13 TOWER; OPEN PARAPETS; PINNACLES; HUGE WINDOWS; FLYING BUTTRESSES; HEXAGONAL PORCH RICHLY CARVED ETC. "THE FAIREST GOODLIEST MOST FAMOUS PARISH CH IN THE KINGDOM" Q. ELIZ I. SHEILA R. & I ARRIVED 1984 TOO LATE FOR THE ANNUAL RUSH BEARING CEREMONY, BY MISCHANCE.

C13 CAPITAL

WELLS delightful small city at foot of Mendip Hills. Phyll H, Sue J, Peggy M, & I often visited from Wedmore 1943 Painting Course. Cathedral? That double branching stair, the inverted nave arches, carved capitals etc are as captivating now, 1984, as then, also those bell ringing clever swans on the Palace moat. I WAS GRANTED A PRIVATE VISIT TO MY LIZARD, CLOSED FOR DECOR.

W. FRONT COVERED FOR REPAIR.

BRUNEL'S CLIFTON SUSPENSION BRIDGE ACROSS THE AVON GORGE 1836 - 64. 245' ABOVE HIGH WATER. WHAT TALES OF FOLK JUMPING FROM IT! I LIVED NEAR, IN A REGENCY TERRACE, & LOVED DOWNLAND WALKS ABOVE THE GORGE, and Cycling out to Chewton Mendip [frid stool] Compton Martin [twisted pillar.]

EACH OF THE MANY PORCH CARVINGS HAS LOCAL PORTRAIT QUALITY.

"Come forth and bring with you a heart, That watches & receives." FRANCIS BACON 1581-1626

THIS & THAT IN SHROPSHIRE, HEREFORDSHIRE, & COTSWOLDS.

1936 "We must find Offa's Dyke & travel the Mary Webb & A.E. Housman country," & Mary R plunged at once into plans for a Youth Hostel walk & wander from Shrewsbury to Chepstow, & Cotswolds. I collected inch maps without which one might well miss good walking tracks.

MUCH WENLOCK
We first went to see the superb Norman arcade of the Priory, & this carved most expressive 800 yr old

Relief Carving in Marble. [SHOULD LOVE TO SEE AGAIN]

Panel 1160, a triple niche under border rich with flower forms, the lavatorium cloister.

CARVED CORBEL KILPECK

ABBEY DORE GOLDEN VALLEY This beautiful boss C13, much influenced me in carving a group of Refugees.

C.E. Montague wrote:-
"The map is our friend. It makes our perception go further. When confusion threatens, it comes to your aid & shows an approach; tells what you would see in each separate direction & from each high point."

Only a few miles on is the world's first

IRONBRIDGE [which we felt impelled to see.] over the R. Severn.

STOKESAY CASTLE FORTIFIED MANOR HOUSE
I was at once endeared to this castle; long banqueting hall with over-hanging storey set between two stone towers C13, & solar. I long, after 50 yrs, to set eyes on it again.

So, well provided against all eventualities, we set off, [BAG in my UP TO THE MINUTE divided skirt,] choosing exclusive picnic spots, wandering hither & thither in the happiest companionship. As if shod with velvet we tirelessly sought this & that, here & there. The enchanting days were each too short.

"Geography is about maps, Biography is about chaps." WE LEARNT MUCH ABOUT EACH!

KILPECK NORMAN S. DOOR

THE GREEN MAN This Norman church, set apart, was my ecstatic climax. Sunset & sunrise saw me transfixed or drawing.

1972 We hunted out OFFA'S DYKE & were lucky to find 2 bunks in an attic at LOWER SPOAD FARM, good country fare, & 12 guests round old oak table in rambling farm hse. LOVELY!

NORMAN GATEHOUSE

HEREFORD 3 CHOIRS FESTIVAL & WORCESTER & GLOUCESTER EVERY 3RD YEAR

OF MONNOW BRIDGE over R. Monnow, MONMOUTH, well known, but unique & had to be drawn.

LUDLOW CARVINGS SEE OPP. PAGE

W. GATE. CHEPSTOW ON WYE, has also wall remains, & a Norman Castle C13 Chapel

ST BRIAVELS CASTLE
I was thrilled 1936 to be Youth Hostelling in this castle with views of the Wye valley.

From Bristol, APRIL 1944, M.M.B & I set off by train, NOT crossing Severn by Aust Ferry, NO SUSPENSION BRIDGE TILL 1965, for a long w. end roaming on the BLACK MTS. Our first lunch picnic; she asked, "What's in yr sandwiches? "Lard," I said "Hobson's choice." She, was wolfing a real fresh hen's egg given by country friend. "Necessity is the Mother of Invention, I suppose," she said. "Sweet are the uses of adversity," I rejoined, & gambolled away up the hill to prove my point. In 1972 from Hay-on-Wye, [WHAT AN ERRATIC RIVER IT IS!] we drove the Border Country, & managed eventually to seek out Gwyneth D, [our neighbour's] dear little wedding church steeply up & alone on the green hill, LLANGYNIEW.

PAINSWICK GABLES
Just the tiniest memory; hillside; stocks; yews; stone houses; & hill viewpoint. A pity no room for other charming Cotswold villages.

BRASS FOUNDER'S TOMB

TINTERN ABBEY Cistercian C12–C14 lies in a bend of the River Wye A very picturesque spot, very Wordsworth ian.

MISERICORD CARVING "BATTERED HUSBAND!
FAIRFORD CHURCH
My bony knees rebelled at so many amusing misericords! Lots of interest both without as well as within, here in this church

BLUE DEVIL STAINED GLASS

Mary Webb's "Precious Bane" greatly illuminated the wild stretches of Stiperstones & Long Mynd for me; & Housman, Wenlock Edge. Malvern Hills, Black Mts, these Welsh Border Hills, each characteristic & good for rambling & exploring.
* THIS WHOLE WALKING TOUR IS TO BE COMPARED WITH A CORONET OF GEMS, A GARLAND OF FLOWERS. AND SO TO BED.

OXFORD & AROUND.

My first visit to the renowned University City of Oxford
"sweet city of dreaming spires"
gave me introduction, intimate & magical, to fritillaries
growing modestly in the water meadows, 1929.

FRITILLARIES so camouflaged, demure, modest, exquisite.

Since then, Maida Stanier of Magdalen College Sch.
has written her books:- POEMS ABOUT OXFORD, THE SINGING TIME etc; I have bathed
deliciously in the soft waters of the Cherwell R.
which flows thro' her garden; my friend M.M.B
has fallen into those waters while punting her
VI th formers in their first sight seeing
tour of Oxford!

POT ON TRIVET OVER FAGGOTS. 1447 [REMEMBER 3 STORY PORCH OF READER'S HOUSE]
Surely the cosiest of misericords LUDLOW P. CHURCH. January.

I have pondered wonderingly in the
college courts NOT ALL 34 OF THEM! dipping into their
history & association with great literary
figures; have enjoyed galleries,
museums, & antique shops,
squandering cash on
desirable brooches to
satisfy a craving,
& compensate for all
those looted in
the London blitz.

BUT NO ANTIQUE
BROOCH COMPARES
WITH THE
ALFRED JEWEL

MAGDALEN TOM TOWER CHRIST CHURCH RADCLIFFE CAMERA OXFORD

DOROTHY WADHAM 1610
HERTFORD COLL. BRIDGE
which I crossed daily for 2 weeks in 1979 while visiting surrounding GREAT HOUSES with Edinburgh Univ.- it reminds of St John's Cambridge, as Carfax quarter boys recall Rye. During many visits to Oxford, Botanic Gdn & fine gate have been enjoyed, but I've never coincided with May sunrise hymns from Magdalen Coll Tower, or Eights week.

CHASTLETON DOOCOT
A most intriguing House, but, coming from Scotland, decided to draw this robust 4 gabled job with lantern cupola

I found this hill top town very bleak on my 1st visit, preferring the Guitings, Slaughters, Bourton on the water, etc.
STOW MKT CROSS

IN GLOUCESTER CATHEDRAL
MISERICORD
THE FALLING PRENTICE
HUNTSMAN BLOWS HIS HORN

CURIOUS PREHISTORIC WHITE HORSE UFFINGTON
How vividly I recall the Oxford to Uffington brain, & that bracing & hilarious RIDGEWAY walk with Phyllis F. & MMB 1949.

IFFLEY NORMAN CHURCH 1170
Astonishing W. Front splendid tower & C12 black slate font, well worth the 2ml walk from Magdalen Bridge. 1929

ON RAILWAY STATION JULY 28 1984 OFF TO SEA SIDE

GLOUCESTER
The Cathedral's vaulted cloister was my earliest architectural thrill, 1929. Since then each visit in turn substantiates that joy, & today's has added the glory of glass & carvings in cartels of Cloister 1984, & en route for Scotland, I enjoy the Golfer E WINDOW CRECY 1350
AND THE QUAYSIDE OF THIS INLAND PORT. 3 CHOIRS MUSIC FESTIVAL
TEWKESBURY MUCH ENJOYED TOO

14 GLASS

IN DORCHESTER ABBEY C14. "You must see the Dorchester Knight for pure essence & simplicity of form," my tutor advised. I was engaged in one year's sculpture study. The Jesse window figure sculptures in the tracery are unusual.
DORCHESTER, & WITTENHAM CLUMPS, CHILTERNS 9mls S from Oxford

Alfred caused me to be late for lunch!
My absorption in this consummate work

ASHMOLEAN MUSEUM [FOUND 1695] N. NEWTON

ROOF OF LETTER BOX

CHELTENHAM SPA
1936, I cycled from Bedford to join the field camping contingent of the World Educational conference; & admired then the Promenade. Today 1984, I've paid attention to Victorian letter boxes, & the Regency ironwork, & canopies of balconies. What grace! What distinction & gentility!
AND WHAT WILD FLOWERS ON THAT COTSWOLD CYCLE ROUTE! SWISS!

JESSE FIGURE COPIED FROM MY BATTERED OLD SKETCHES & I LONG TO VISIT & DRAW AGAIN & SEE THAT LEAD NORMAN FONT.
BRACKET FIGURE MONK RESTING

CHERWELL THAMES

"What shelter to grow ripe is ours
What leisure to grow wise." M. ARNOLD

SOME NOTES ARISING FROM SHORT VISITS TO THE N. MIDLANDS.

Chester is one of my favourite cities with its ancient walls & towers, its unique Rows [which are pedestrian precincts] & its Abbey Church, now Cathedral, with those exciting choir stall carvings. The 3 red sandstone spires of _Lichfield_ Cathedral 'LADIES OF THE VALE' are a compelling sight. The richly carved W. Front makes tremendous impact. The cobbled Mkt Sq; the associations with Dr Johnson & Ashmole; the 8 chimneys of St John's Hospital; the Minster Pool, & the Stowe Pool all combine to give this city its distinction.

Enid C. lives in Chester. We have resumed a friendship of girlhood after 60 yrs silence. Delys B. lives near Lichfield. We revived contact after 30 yrs silence on a chance meeting Oslo. Cecily F. lives near Tarporley. We were together for 2 weeks in Thailand & meet occasionally. VISITING THESE WELCOMING FRIENDS HAS OPENED MY EYES TO THEIR LOCAL COUNTRYSIDES.

TAPESTRY, GLASS, EPSTEIN'S SCULPTURE.

COVENTRY CATHEDRAL made me wonder, as did Lady Godiva - peeping Tom in childhood days; but how much more deeply today!

1942, A SHEFFIELD ANTIQUARY PROVIDED THESE TWO TREASURES, CARVED IVORY TUSKS IN THIS TIME OF DEPRESSION. Then, Mr R & I were at a Drama Course - what a changed Sheffield 1984! when our own Coach, Harrogate to Buxton, passed through. 4"

Was sorry to miss seeing my friend Elma C, but we managed to glimpse in passing the LOCKUP on Bastow Bridge over R. Derwent with its merciful louvres. SUBSTANTIAL! YES! BUILT TO LAST. HOW LONG. ??

80 yr old seeks help from schoolgirl:- "Is that a crown on the steeple?" "Is my contact lenses in." "Sorry, I haven't English" young man, I no speak "young lady; "It's so high, & I hate a very stiff neck." "I MUST REMEMBER MY BINOCULARS IN FUTURE & BE INDEPENDENT!

I am addicted to looking upwards, as is my pen-friend Irma I, ["MIND YOU DON'T TRIP!!" FOLK SAY] not only to skeins of geese, flying high to the skimming swallows, winter tree traceries, diving gulls, & swinging masts;

LOCKUP, NEAR BAKEWELL

IN CHESTER
The elderlies walked the 2+ miles of the wall with vigour, sketching the towers & the Eastgate Bridge Clock, then off to spy out the Cathedral choir carvings enriching the pews.

I'd like to have been a medieval carver making such an individual benchend as this.

INVERNESS

W. WEMYSS

BLEDINGTON

WATSON'S EDINB.

3 OF THE PEW END CARVINGS

THE PILGRIM; STUDENT NUN;

CURIOUS FIGURE WITH TANKARD

"THE KING HIMSELF IS SERVED BY THE FIELD"
"THE PROFIT OF THE EARTH IS FOR ALL"
TWO TEXTS BENEATH MUSICIAN FIGURES ABOVE A SHOP FRONT

JACOB'S DREAM.

BUT ALSO TO:- gables & eaves, finials & cornices, spires & minarets, skyline sculptures, weather vanes, chimney stacks, etc all those top knots & visual excitements missed when one is engaged upon the daily round & common task of getting & spending.

THUS MY LETTER CARDS WERE ENTITLED:- "THE LOOK UP SERIES."

SHEFFIELD P.H. OFFICIAL
ECCLESIASTIC
ENDULARLY PRESBYTERIAN
GARGOYLE

"Look round, look up, and feel a moment's space, That carpet dusting, tho' a pretty trade, Is not the imperative labour after all" E.B.B.

LICHFIELD CATHEDRAL

"3 LADIES OF THE VALE" RISE ABOVE TREES OF THE CATHEDRAL CLOSE

EXQUISITE SCREEN. G. SCOTT

A 2 hour lunch break from the coach en route for Edinburgh was my chance to see Lichfield, the Pools, Johnson Museum, etc with picnic, before entering the Cathedral with the party.

CHATSWORTH a Great House indeed, impressive in every way, & such water gardens! Yet all I drew was this coil of mounted household keys & the boars. [HARDWICK HALL I MUST REVISIT to REFRESH A VERY EARLY BLURRED MEMORY]

FOLLOW ME / PEACE TO ALL PEOPLE / WATER OF LIFE

Tewkesbury Abbey was depicted recently

DERBYSHIRE WELL DRESSING
EARLY SUMMER SEES THIS REMARKABLE CUSTOM OF BLESSING THE WELLS IN FULL SWING

FLOWER PETAL MOSAICS IN 8-10 FOOT FRAMES DEPICT MOSTLY BIBLICAL THEMES, TITLE & BORDERS

MANY WILLING HANDS WORK THE INTRICATE DESIGNS FOR MANY HOURS & DAYS, NOW DONE IN AID OF CHARITIES.

WE CHECKED THE VARIOUS VILLAGE DATES WELL IN ADVANCE.

RAVENNA MOSAICS CAME TO BRITAIN 1946? & STARTED A FASHION. SEEDS, PEBBLES, STAMPS, SHARDS, STRINGS, ETC USED

"Good company, & good discourse are the very sinews of virtue" IZAAK WALTON 1593-1683
VERY DISAPPOINTING THERE WAS NO OPPORTUNITY TO ENJOY YOURS, CHRISTINE.

MEMENTOES. YORKSHIRE DALES.

DETAIL CANALETTO in the astonishing BOWES MUSEUM.

PACK HORSE BELL

GOOD CLOG EXHIBIT

BUTTER MARKERS

IN HAWES MUSEUM. STILES ON THE PENNINE WAY

BARNARD CASTLE ON TEES. 3 sculptured musicians on BLAGRAVES HSE, ANCIENT CASTLE, BRIDGE, 2 STOREY COLONADED HALL, BOWES MUSEUM.

Wet Sunday morn at AYSGARTH FALLS, URE. Saw oak carved Scott & Hero in the Parish Ch from JERVAULX ABBEY

GAINFORD VILLAGE ON TEES. Gracious & tranquil. Village green, th. porch, leisured fishermen; idyllic setting.

Cheap November Rail Travel is a welcome boon & a cheerful stimulus to the elderly.

I think of the enterprising 92 yr old Tynesider who will spend all the year studying time tables & maps to work out plans for rail travel each day of November!

It may well give a bonus as it did to me, when by the greatest good fortune Nancy D. & I PERFECT STRANGERS, tuned in on a journey Darlington to London. Subsequently her kind hospitality in Gainford & that of her friend Esther S. in Richmond have given me pleasant days in the DALES later extended by the open invitation of those friends Pat & Cyril R. of Wensleydale whom I met in Morocco

SUCH SERENDIPITY, NEVER SOUGHT & RARELY BESTOWED, IS JOYFUL WHEN IT CHANCES TO OCCUR!

We fumbled STRAIGHT ON! our way across THE WAY? heathery wastes, a sombre landscape, industrial valleys, to climb at last up the stone paved hill of HAWORTH, past the graveyard to the Brontë home, poignant with memories.

SPINNERS LONGRIDGE BISHOPSDALE. What a sociable occupation with good end product! In Laura Drake's 1653 farmhouse up on hillside Pat Kent joins 10 other spinner enthusiasts monthly 1985

Back in April 1954, motoring the Dales in our new Morris;— "We must try it out on the Buttertubs Pass" said M: M:B, & up on the top we took a picnic. Not a soul used that empty road as we sat munching food & view! Some 30 mls later WHERE WAS MY HANDBAG? Back we climbed, passing no soul, no car, but ALAS! no bag at the picnic spot. 3 WEEKS LATER, back home in London, there, sitting on the table was my h. bag intact, delivered by police, no charge & no obligation. WHO HAD FOUND IT? A Sea Cadet with his unit crossing the moors on exercise spotted a dark object 'queening the Pass' MY HANDBAG! He would accept no reward but drooled over the book of poems which I sent & I drooled over his reply. A sparkling, jolly correspondence ensued, without sequel.

IRON & GLASS STREET CANOPY, ELEGANT, LATE, IN HARROGATE

MISERICORD

13 WALL PAINTINGS EASBY OS P.CHURCH with the Abbey, a rural scene of beauty

MISERICORDS FROM ABBEY now in RICHMOND P CHURCH

EASBY & RICHMOND

BY RIPON CARVERS? POPULAR DANCING PIGS.

I spotted these curious roof tiles with disbelief. Maimie T's kind hospitality gave us a centre for Haworth, Knaresborough, Bolton Abbey, Harewood House etc

MISERICORDS

A lovely town, the fine setting a knockout as one approaches; castle dramatic on its cliff; the SWALE swirling turbulently round; the cobbled Market Place, extensive, sloping, & with Obelisk, tiny Georgian Theatre 1788 [Ellen Terry, Edmund Kean etc]

BISHOP'S SYMBOL OF POWER. BENCH END.

RIPON

How merciful that I can still squat down to discover & finger details of these strange cryptic carvings of Cathedral stalls.

"SWEET ESPECIAL RURAL SCENE" How often I recalled these words as we met Leyburn [The Shawl] Wensley, Wittons, W. Burton, Kettlewell, Hubberholm, Thornton Rust, Buttertubs, Thwaite, Keld, Muker, Healaugh, Grinton Cath of etc Dales.

"Acquaintance I would have — when it depends Not on the number, but the choice of friends." A. Cowley 1660

IN LAKELAND

Oh! the Lakeland walks, scrambles, climbs we had, Mary R. & I !!

[We met by chance at a London School of Drama Course 55 yrs ago, & since then have developed an enduring lifelong friendship]

From Newcastle, HER HOME TOWN, she introduced me to these, my very first 1935 mountain tops, Scawfell & Langdale Pikes, Gable, Striding Edge etc.

Ecstatic, elevating it certainly was, & rapturous, looking down on to the Lakes from above. But bathing in them NAKED SKIN TO COLD WATER after a climb was indeed exhilarating.

We could do this in those early days, specially in Crummock EUIDH TOO.

A civilised TEA, a change after picnics! In 'OLD ENGLAND HOTEL' WINDERMERE 1984 Thank you Daphne.

RON WHITESIDE

RAIN?

Yes! 1942 gave us 2 weeks of it in daily grey drenchings, determined & unabating; Stonethwaite.

We didn't care We accepted the inevitable!

We donned macs & wellies & sloshed around for exercise, or stayed inside to read, write, draw, sew, tat, or practise the art of theatrical makeup

BEATRIX POTTER SAWREY

WE SPOTTED NAPES NEEDLE ON OUR WASDALE STYE HEAD PASS WALK.

ROCK CLIMBERS? NO!

PACKS TODAY 1986

EYES. HAWK? HEN HARRIER? CLARAMARA EAGLE?

Achieving Red Pike Remember? 1941 Euidh

ALF, JIM.

Mrs Whiteside who gave us a Cumbrian Home Baked Farm Tea Groaning table 1941

LETTERS TO HUGH WALPOLE FROM:-
A. Bennett
T.E. Lawrence
S. Maugham
Chas Morgan
V. Woolf
J. Epstein
J. Conrad
J. Galsworthy
M. Beerbohm
J. Masefield
O. Sitwell
H. James
W. De La Mare

GRASMERE
DOVE COTTAGE

E.A.K. 1770

SPICE CUPBOARD

WORDSWORTH'S PORTMANTEAU

RYDAL MOUNT

KESWICK an intriguing little town, black & white Town House, surrounded by Fells, a Mecca to climbers. I spent a wet afternoon enthralled by letters & manuscripts.

A MEMORY

R: SOUTHEY'S FLUTE, WOOD, IVORY, SILVER. HE LIVED IN KESWICK. LETTERS, & FLUTE IN 'KESWICK MUSEUM'

"Now stir the fire, & close the shutters fast;
Let fall the curtains, wheel the sofa round
And, while the bubbling and loud hissing urn
Throws up a steamy column, and the cups
That cheer but not inebriate wait on each,
So let us welcome peaceful evening in."
W. COWPER

Now in 1985, Dorothy G. has again extended the hospitality of her beautiful home with its panorama of Lakeland Hills. These we still enjoy in contemplative retrospect.

FELL RUNNERS GRASMERE SPORTS

SOME EVOCATIVE NAMES:-
Helvellyn
Great Dod
High Seat
Derwent
Causey Pike
Brackenthwaite
Grisedale Pike
Whinlatter
Crummock
Buttermere
High Stile
Red Pike
Stake Pass
Great End
Glaramara
Honister
Scarth Gap
Pillar
Steeple

GRANDY NOOK HAWKSHEAD

THE PIG & WHISTLE NOW RED LION INN

CHIMNEY GRANDY NOOK

HAWKSHEAD, a romantic village; 2 squares cobbled streets in a confusion of directions. All very appealing. WORDSWORTH ASSOCIATIONS AGAIN.

After the wide flowing lines of the Pennine Chain, the approach to this close packed press & dense conglomeration of monster humps is breathtaking, challenging.

"KNOW A COUNTRY THROUGH THE SOLES OF YOUR BOOTS" is said with gd advice

Hill country regions each have their own distinct individuality & Lakeland Hills are quite different from those of the West Highlands.

DERWENT WATER

"What a rush & crush of mountain profiles do rise clamouring here"

"To cut across the shadow of a star That gleamed across the ice" W.W.
ICE SKATING ON ESTHWAITE.

Level valleys & narrow lakes serve to heighten the effect of their containing mountains.

"What is an epigram? A dwarfish whole Its body brevity, & wit its soul." S.T.C.

IN NORTHUMBRIA

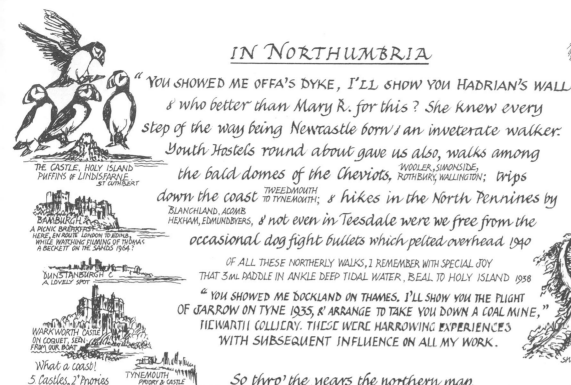

"YOU SHOWED ME OFFA'S DYKE, I'LL SHOW YOU HADRIAN'S WALL" & who better than Mary R. for this? She knew every step of the way being Newcastle born & an inveterate walker. Youth Hostels round about gave us also, walks among the bald domes of the Cheviots, WOOLER, SIMONSIDE, ROTHBURY, WALLINGTON; trips down the coast TWEEDMOUTH TO TYNEMOUTH; & hikes in the North Pennines by BLANCHLAND, ACOMB HEXHAM, EDMUNDBYERS, & not even in Teesdale were we free from the occasional dog fight bullets which pelted overhead 1940

OF ALL THESE NORTHERLY WALKS, I REMEMBER WITH SPECIAL JOY THAT 3ML PADDLE IN ANKLE DEEP TIDAL WATER, BEAL TO HOLY ISLAND 1938

"YOU SHOWED ME DOCKLAND ON THAMES. I'LL SHOW YOU THE PLIGHT OF JARROW ON TYNE 1935, & ARRANGE TO TAKE YOU DOWN A COAL MINE," HEWARTH COLLIERY. THESE WERE HARROWING EXPERIENCES WITH SUBSEQUENT INFLUENCE ON ALL MY WORK.

THE CASTLE, HOLY ISLAND. PUFFINS OF LINDISFARNE. ST CUTHBERT

BAMBURGH. A PICNIC BREAKFAST HERE, EN ROUTE LONDON TO EDINB, WHILE WATCHING FILMING OF THOMAS A BECKETT ON THE SANDS 1964?

DUNSTANBURGH C. A LOVELY SPOT

WARKWORTH CASTLE ON COQUET, SEEN FROM OUR BOAT

What a coast! 5 Castles, 2 Priories good beaches, & my first east coast fishing villages 1934. I was caught & enthralled by these. Beadnell's neat little harbour had to be drawn, & Crasters tasty kippers relished, & sent as presents.

TYNEMOUTH PRIORY & CASTLE

MARY GRIMALKIN PUSS

3 ROMAN DEITIES!

HADRIAN'S WALL APRIL 1934. Good weather in Newcastle, so off we went by train for HOUSESTEADS. But alas, capricious fickle day. Mist overhung the WALL. Only fitful bursts of brightness as we snaked our way along the ridge.

So thro' the years the northern map, & the Geordies, & that very enterprising Newcastle People's Theatre became a great eye opener to me. And how much vitality there is in Newcastle today!

4 GRISLY HEADS AT WALLINGTON, once on London Wall— ballast for ships [N.T. 1941] London to N/castle. Sir Chas. Trevelyan's. Stately Home had traditions of public service. We frequently used its Youth Hostel & enthused over w/end schools there 1930's.

A mighty entrance, narrow, tall, monumental, I recalled Mycenae! the Percy Stronghold! James Johnson (18 had fun designing these alert dutiful roof sentinels, but a cold day for drawing them DEC 12 1984. A spectacular castle & very attractive gated town on the Aln.

ALNWICK CASTLE C14 BARBICAN

Thank you Joan B for adding to it with your distinctive paintings. How fortunate that we each introduced ourselves in Samarkand!

When I first came, 1934, Youth Hostelling in these parts, such remote, wild and wide open fell country was new to me. I had to tune in to it. With what astonishment we witnessed the birth of an unsteady little lamb on the hillside

PRIOR LEISCHMAN'S CHANTRY TOMB CARVINGS VERY CURIOUS

HEXHAM ABBEY CHURCH SEE ALSO PAGE 46

HEXHAM ON TYNE. Market Square; Moot Hall (12 Gatehouse; (14 Manor Office [WALL]; Columned Shelter (18, & Abbey Church all group pleasantly. The coup d'oeil for me:- the lancet windows of N. Transept as you enter Abbey church. BLANCHLAND, COMPACT STONE VILLAGE ON DERWENT SET BETWEEN HIGH FELLS, IS A HAVEN.

NIGHT STAIR

ALNMOUTH. From the railway this looks to be & is an alluring little town. I find it both charming & tranquil. quite a retreat, 3-4 mls from Alnwick.

SUPERB LANTERN TOWER ST. NICHOLAS CATH. NEWCASTLE ON TYNE

ST. CUTHBERT'S JEWELLED PECTORAL CROSS DURHAM CITY

Both these cities crammed with interest SEE IN "GLIMPSES OF CITIES AT HOME & ABROAD"

Kilted Magi greet Virgin & child in this remote village KIRKNEWTON church & unusual (12 & 13 parts.

Geordies 1940
"People have one thing in common: they are all different." Bob ZEND

IN YORKSHIRE & HEXHAM

FARNDALE DAFFS & SNOW 1978

THREE DIARY ENTRIES:-
APRIL 1947. Off to Helmsley, MMB & I with bikes [by train London to York.]
JUNE 1977. Off to York to see Jane & Richard from Bristol [train Edinb to York.]
OCTOBER 1982. Off to York to see Jennifer S. from B.Stortford [ditto with joy!]

We all learnt much about Monasticism, Orders, sublime impressive architecture. the Carthusians of KIRKHAM PRIORY

1947 — HELMSLEY MKT TOWN — DW R.RYE
1947 AT BLACK SWAN
1978 SUTHERLAND LODGE HOTEL CROPTON 1978

Since those 3 diary entries several visits have endeared me to this Queen of Cities.

My enchantment with the City itself gave a good excuse for joining the 1985 Edinburgh University Extra Mural Tour 'Abbeys & Priories of Yorkshire.'

COXWOLD — L. STERNE TRISTRAM SHANDY
My first N.Yorks village of so many charmers- Hawnby, Hutton le Hole, Thornton, Lastingham etc

INTRINSIC BEAUTY
FOUNTAINS Cistercian Abbey set in the parkland of STUDLEY ROYAL, lakes, ponds, woodland, no wonder artists flocked to draw this superb ruin.

We visited Finchale, Kirkham & Mount Grace Priories; the Abbeys of Byland, Rievaulx, & Fountains, Whitby, & Hexham; York Minster, Ripon Cathedral, learning much about Monastic Orders & monkhood

RIEVAULX How I've enjoyed a leg stretching walk along grass terrace from temple to temple, before plunging steeply to those majestic Abbey ruins below, to exult, muse, & draw.

A TRAVESTY IT MAY BE, IT MAY BE 15 MINS OF PURE JOY TO ME

We were based in the COLLEGE OF RIPON & YORK ST.JOHN & fattened on the sumptuous menus of food prepared daily for us there. Our enthusiasm for food & for Abbeys knew no bounds. Joyous laughter helped digestion! Even Una, our lively energetic vegetarian was lavishly fed!

WHITBY. The Abbey, [spotted beyond radomes OF FILINGDALES] makes an incongruous sight. Close to, spectacular on its high cliff, 199 steps up to it! from attractive harbours River Esk, & sands. St Mary's Church, a period piece of gt interest. HOW TO STOP DRAWING I DID NOT KNOW!!

3 TIER PULPIT — PARISH CHURCH OF ST MARY

BLANCHLAND FIRST MET IN 1954 a magnet for a detour- Thus a Stone village, unique, nestled in the moors, on our way to

CRYPT — FRITH STOOL OF SANCTUARY BISHOP'S THRONE?

BYLAND ABBEY C12 Cistercian ruins Water leaf capitals, Mosaic tiled floors in black & white & green.

CHOIR SCREEN PAINTED C14 BEAUTIFUL ECCLESIASTICS & APOSTLES ETC.

HEXHAM, always a good port of call en route for Edinb. I never tire of visiting the Abbey etc & today entered the Saxon Crypt. ST WILFRID

The County of Yorkshire is celebrated for so much that the TUSSLE between words & drawings for SPACE is ever present. All must be sifted for a place, all must be pruned & tailored, sketches greatly reduced, & dovetailed, & much regretfully discarded.

'A PAGE MUST BREATHE', it is said. I try, but often fail to obey this dictum.

MISERICORD ST.WILFRID WHEELS AGED MOTHER
RIPON
SAMSON
We all went along to hear the HORN BLOWING by that jolly Wakeman 9.0 p.m. from 'FOURE CORNERS OF THE CROSSE' I spent afternoon hours grovelling on bruised knees entranced with misericords THEN TO THE REMARKABLE CRYPT SAXON

HANDS IN PAINTINGS ART GALLERY

THE CITY OF YORK * has everything, from boats on its R. Ouse, stout walls, bars & bastions, medieval streets to its superlative Minster with glorious Chapter Hse C13. A non pareil. No wonder folk flock. My best visits have been in Dec. & Jan! * SEE MORE IN "CITIES & COUNTRYSIDES AT HOME & ABROAD."

"....Life piled on life Were all too little, and of one to me Little remains" said Ulysses. A.T
'SO ENJOY EACH DAY' SAY I

"By the hammer & the hand, all arts do stand" [INN, HUTTON LE HOLE.]

E. RIDING, LINCOLN, SOUTHWELL, PETERBORO!

MKT CROSS

Coincidence, 20·6·84
In the train south from Edinburgh [I WAS IDLY DRAWING] my seat companion MALE said:- "I'm sure you're the lady I saw on television last week; you draw & scribe don't you?" We talked. Later: "My daughter gets married soon. Would you consider designing the wedding card?" The mother of that bride turned out to be an erstwhile 'student' friend of mine!   COINCIDENCES ABOUND!

N·GATE

BEVERLEY, SUCH AN INVITING TOWN, FRIENDLY STN MASTER, MKT CROSS, N·GATE IN BRICK, FRIARY YOUTH HOSTEL, SQUARES, ST MARY'S CH. WITH MINSTREL PILLAR, & MINSTER. "THE MUSICAL MINSTER" I CALL IT FOR THOSE DELIGHTFUL MUSICIAN CARVINGS, A MINSTER THAT REJOICES! FRID STOOL

ST·MARYS BRIDLINGTON

A prized possession:- Priory nave, rich N. porch, huge window above W door; black carv'd grave slab. Lovely resort, wish I'd sketched attractive harbour.

I was on the way to Andrea L. another 'student' friend, with her musical children, in Lincoln. Never shall I forget the impact of those 3 Cathedral towers LINCOLN, soaring up, triumphant, from the hill which itself reigns supreme on the wide open sea of waving corn. Unforgettable also, the twin towers of Beverley Minster, resplendent, glowing, in the westering winter sunlight.

SCARBOROUGH
I GLIMPSED THIS RENOWNED RESORT BETWEEN TRAINS FROM A TAXI "A PAUSE FOR 2 MINUTE SKETCH" I REQUESTED, & AT ONCE UNDERSTOOD ITS ACCLAIM; HILLS, 2 BAYS, SANDS, CASTLE MARINE DRIVE, ETC. COINCIDENCE: THE CRAWFORDS IN MY NEXT TRAIN!

In Bridlington I visit my friend Phyll H. Her "ivory tower" is a unique sight. Walls lined with cupboards of tiny dimensions, pull out shelves, little boxes, drawers, full of labelled trifles; an Aladdin's cave of curios; a museum & library which transports me magic carpet wise to distant lands.

P's trifles; stones, eggs, fossils, batik, dyes, horse brasses, etc. recalled Janet P's fond addiction to dolls, & to attic cupboards! BOTH OF THEM FERVENT ENTHUSIASTS.

✷ LINCOLN

History lives on this limestone hill rising steeply above the plain. A favoured spot through all the ages, the enormous Cathedral a knockout spectacle reigning supreme in this fine city, castle battlements & towers give wide views. Lincoln is a vivid & singular experience.

ANGEL EXPELS ADAM & EVE [LINCOLN ANGELS]

DOMESTIC BRAWL MISERICORD

DIARY ENTRY, BRIDLINGTON 1972:-
Marie & Rachel of THORNTON-LE-DALE just returned from Ispahan, Shiraz, Persepolis, persuade "Go now," they say, "you'll never regret it." But sadly we did not 'GRASP THE SKIRTS OF HAPPY CHANCE,' & now it is impossible.

A MEMORY OF OUR CLIFF WALK, FLAMBOROUGH, 17.8.85, PHYLL, JO, DOG, ME.

Crawling among Lincoln Cath choir stalls, torch in hand, I collided with another misericord addict. We chatted sotto voce on our knees. "For carving go to Southwell," don't miss it" he urged. Under what odd circumstances one can associate, & under what adverse conditions one often draws;- frost bite; needling mist; boisterous wind; party disappearing; companion edgy; subject moving; time pressing; vehicle in motion; & oh! spectators gathering! COURAGE MON AMI, LE DIABLE EST MORT.

CARVINGS IN SOUTHWELL MINSTER

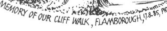

TWO RINGED BULL GARGOYLES   RAM

2 CAPITALS

BOAR EATS ACORNS   MAPLE & POTENTILLA

✷ PETERBOROUGH CATHEDRAL

So powerful, so profound in conception, such robust dignity, that I feel tremendous awe & praise on entering, eyes trained on those distinguished & distinctive wooden vaults.
✷✷ MORE DETAILS IN "GLIMPSES OF CITIES & COUNTRYSIDES AT HOME & ABROAD."

HEADS WELL SWATHED YET MINI KILTS!

CARVED MISERICORD. [UNISEX?] LOVERS

HUMBER BRIDGE, SEEN FROM TRAIN TO BEVERLEY LONGEST SINGLE SPAN BGE IN WORLD, 1981.

"Wherein lies happiness? In that which becks Our ready minds to fellowship ----- J. KEATS

EAST ANGLIA, NORTHERLY.

Angel roofs first drew me with curiosity to these parts, [& what an inspiration they are!] also bird watching, & the Norfolk Broads; but when I got as far as Norwich in the east, & Ely in the west, my enthusiasm knew no bounds.

GODWIT

AVOCET MINSMERE TITCHWELL HAVERGATE

CURLEW BLACKWATER OLD HALL MARSHES

ST. WENDREDA MARCH.

THE MAGNIFICENT VAULT ANGEL CARVINGS WHICH I HAVE TO VISIT YET AGAIN & THIS TIME WITH BINOCULARS!

BLYTHBOROUGH

WITH STARS

WYMONDHAM VAULT

SPANGLED

1713 CLEY NEXT SEA

The Post Office was my magnet!

BURNHAM OVERY [YACHTING]

TOWER MILL

W. Mills are still a feature of the E.A. landscape, "sailing boats on fields" NORFOLK BROADS.

CLARE. Just an approx note of the PARGETING on this most attractive house. Such plaster decor is an E Anglian feature.

Norwich is a special magnet. Ordering a café coffee one day [& remarking upon the weather,] my table companion [a Scot & stranger] chatted. "I seem to recognise your voice." [I have a slight lisp] "Were you on Radio Forth & B.B.C Book Programs recently? I've bought your books, being a calligrapher myself. Perhaps you'd sign them if we did meet again?" MORE SERENDIPITY! THEY SAY THE WORLD IS SMALL, YES!

SWAFFHAM MKT CROSS 1783

A town to explore. Many elegant houses, Assembly Room Very Regency. "A rural Montpelier". Angel roof of church most inspiring (s. legendary Swaffham Pedlar.

N. WALSHAM MKT. CROSS V. UNUSUAL

3 TIERS CLOCK TURRET 8 OAK COLUMNS COCK WINDVANE

WALSINGHAM WIND VANE ABOVE SHRINE OF OUR LADY OF PILGRIMAGE FAME. I MUCH LIKE THIS VILLAGE, ITS AURA, ITS MUSEUM, ST MARY'S CH & VERY SPECIAL FONT, ETC

DEREHAM Bishop Bonner's pargetted Cottages 1502 Cowper monument in church.

DEREHAM TOWN SIGN ACROSS HIGH STREET.

I PSWICH ST MARY LE QUAY [my aunt lived here. 1923 I fainted in HIGH ST!] No room for pargeting on Sparrowe's Hse, NOW BOOKSHOP.

LAVENHAM Timber framed houses transport me to former ages of wool prosperity, the Guildhall Wool Hall & many houses.

WILLY LOTT'S COTTAGE & FLATFORD MILL N.T. N.T.

Constable's boyhood spent here. Now Centre for Field Studies which we much enjoyed.

[LEISTON, SUFFOLK: A.S. NEILL]

DEDHAM CHURCH 1492 We were impressed by the lavish Flower Festivals held under the great roof timbers. CHURCH IN MANY CONSTABLE PTGS.

Now, since Hilda MY SISTER has come to live in Norfolk, visits to this 2nd home have revived contacts with Hazel F., Phyll F.G & other friends of yore.
Wide skies, rural scenes;
sails between fields;
birds by the thousand;
stately homes;
fine churches;
attractive villages;
Gurneys, Frys, Pastons,
Cowper, Sir T. Browne;
East Anglian Painters,
all combine to give these parts
a distinct identity.
"Beauty in things exists in the mind which contemplates them" D. DAVID HUME

"Oh look! stop we must! Very eye catching among much Georgian building

ABBEY GATEWAY 1347 BURY ST EDMUNDS

KINGS LYNN

2 GREAT CHURCHES 2 GUILDHALLS! 2 MARKETPLACES CHEQUERED FLINT FACADE OF OLD GUILDHALL HAD ME ROOTED. K. JOHN'S CUP; SOUTH GATE IMPRESSED. CUSTOM HSE REMINDED OF HISORY. HANSEATIC LEAGUE. F. BURNEY BORN HERE. R. OUSE. HAIL! MARION & FAMILY.

1495 BRASS. "WIFE & DAUGHTERS OF WILLIAM DE GREY." very graceful. MERTON Brasses are underfoot, misericords under seats, both crafts of gt beauty.

HOPI PLANTS VINEYARD BOSS

TUTIVILLUS EAVESDROPS ON GOSSIPS "I AM A POURE DYVEL, TYTYVYLLUS," he filled his sack with scribal errors & verbal atrocities, & later with mumblers, drawlers, yawners, nappers. SO beware!

ELY on OUSE
From the train the Cathedral is seen from miles away across the Fens. Walking uphill from the river we were pregnant with anticipation roundly fulfilled. Our contemplative picnic on the plain, on the Green served to help absorb & digest this rich aesthetic diet, the Lantern Octagon supreme
* SEE ALSO, "GLIMPSES OF CITIES, COUNTRYSIDES AT HOME & ABROAD.

NORWICH, a city with everything. After many 90 visits, I hope for many more. Superb Cathedral, nave vault, regal apse, bosses, misericords; great Keep of Castle, Museums, churches, Madder mkt theatre, & much more. GREETINGS, DAVID & GEMMA.

Feb 1986. KIND ENQUIRY:- "Do you cycle these days? Do you jog? Do you walk?" Yes, all three, & the greatest of these is a leg stretching contemplative walk through a gently rolling countryside. The mind races, the imagination is stirred, the soul replenished. Note pad at hand for the sketching pause.
* SEE ALSO:- "GLIMPSES OF CITIES..." D.A.G.
"Taste your legs, sir; put them to motion." said Sir Toby.

EAST ANGLIA, SOUTHERLY.

My forbears were Suffolk & Essex people, & Essex countryside was the bliss of my childhood days.

How well I remember that first holiday at 7yrs, going from London to my Uncle Arthur BAKER; PURLEIGH NEAR MALDON, & his 8 daughters, ONE SON, away back in 1913. Rapturous it was to be released from town & school worries into flowery lanes & green fields. And, my Uncle John's farm, in Althorne, held a rural magic for me which never faded.

"Heaven lies about us in our infancy"

MY HEAVEN LAY HERE IN THE COUNTRY LIFE OF THESE RURAL VILLAGES & FARMS.

WHAT A FAMILY TO FEED & CLOTHE HELPED BY THE HENS PIGS COWS FRESH AIR. THEY AVOWED.

HOW GOOD THAT MANY VILLAGES HAVE MAYPOLES. WE SAW THIS AT ICKWELL FROM BEDFORD, 1946

In 1947 I planned cycle tours to unearth ancestral records. In those days one could flag down a train from B.Stortford WHERE I WORKED, to stop for me & bike at the Golf Club Halt WHERE I LIVED, to alight at Dunmow, Braintree, Witham etc, & cycle on to remote villages; names proliferate:-

THUNDERSLEY, BURNHAM-ON-CROUCH, BRADWELL ST PETERS, MALDON-ON-BLACKWATER, TOLLESHUNT D'ARCY, GT TOTHAM, BROOMFIELD, W. BERGHOLT, DEDHAM, FLATFORD-ON-STOUR, LAVENHAM, LONG MELFORD, GT. YELDHAM, FINCHINGFIELD, THAXTED, RODINGS, ETC.

THAXTED
A 15 mile cycle ride to see this unbelievable C16 Guildhall, windmill & fine church, so exciting without, & light within

MORRIS DANCERS 1958

FINCHINGFIELD
2 ARTISTS PAINTING WHILE I EXPLORED THIS "DROPPED FROM HEAVEN" VILLAGE. MANY OTHER CHARMERS ABOUT; BARDFIELD, KERSEY, ETC – BUT THIS IS REFLECTED!

"Three ducks on a pond-----"

COGGESHALL
Paycocke's C16 long tasteful house on the main Colchester Rd is most engaging.
I Remember MALDON, scenic above the R. Blackwater, & the yachting at BURNHAM-ON-CROUCH??

W. MERSEA & ITS OYSTER BEDS & SAILING INTEREST REMEMBER?

That boat trip on the Orwell from Ipswich to Felixstowe with my Auntie Kitty was Mother's highly recommended favourite sea trip. 1924

ST. IVES C15 BRIDGE
6 STONE ARCHES & LITTLE CHAPEL FOR TRAVELLERS' PRAYERS. WE COULDN'T STOP, – BUT SHLD LOVE TO GO INSIDE!

SAFFRON WALDEN
ANOTHER CAPTIVATING TOWN, FINE CHURCH; PARGETING, MAZE; MUSEUM, & AUDLEY END MANSION NEAR BY.

SUN INN PLASTER RELIEF

St. Albans was a 2nd home after College days. Friendship with Rene S. Is now 62 yrs old! A job of work at Bedford for 7yrs gave familiarity with those parts. Bishop Stortford was my final seat of work with frequent commuting to London & Cambridge. How many good friends there, not forgetting Betty P. & HER 3 DOGS!

Historic COLCHESTER Do you Remember the thousands of ancient bricks in buildings? in the great Nave & W. door of the Priory, the walls, the huge Keep, its Museum, All Saints, & that hospitable Holly Trees Museum?

W. DOOR (SAXON) HOLY TRINITY

CAMBRIDGE
Frequent meetings here included loitering in Quads, punting the river, wandering the Backs; coffees, & much musing in the elegant stately Fitzwilliam Museum THOUGHTS OF WINIFRED B

Those Rivers, CAM, OUSE, STORT, have each been boated on or swum in' with dragon fly, water lily, & king fisher pleasure.

Do you Remember chatting with Henry Moore, his studio, his garden much Hadham, & that meeting in B. Stortford?

ST. ALBANS
Remember those celebration jaunts? the Cathedral Service; scatter for picnic lunches; the steep hill down to river, lake, & Verulamium?

WALL PAINTING IN NAVE

ROMAN FLOOR MOSAIC VERULAMIUM

"THE GREATEST BOON AFTER GOOD HEALTH IS TO HAVE GOOD FRIENDS."

HOCKERILL COLLEGE
Do you Remember those torchlight Christmas processions, candles in jars, red blankets; round the hospitals & town to end in the Quad; then hot mince pies round roaring fires blazing; Carol Services in All Saints; Xmas Dinner & Plays; Going Down Dinner; Stage Plays; Projects; T. Practices; Problems UGH!

GREETINGS TO:-
Heather M; Peggy C; Nigel W; Jocelyn D; Hazel F; Joan R; Thelma H; Patricia A; Margaret D; Sheila H; Janet B;

"I count myself in nothing else so happy"
"As in a soul remembering my good friends" W. SH.

THESE E. ANGLIAN RIVERS & THE BEDFORD OUSE HAVE GIVEN FUN & RELAXATION WITH FLEETING KINGFISHER GLIMPSES.

Margaret S; Maggie C; Margaret L; Judy H; Ann B; Stella B; Janet M; Edna C; Mary M; Muriel M'G; Ray S; Eric R; David C; Alice E.

FIRESIDES

"*All our adventures were at the fireside*" O. Goldsmith
1730-1774

"To make a happy fireside clime
For weans and wife,
That's the true pathos & sublime
Of human life." ROBERT BURNS
1759-1796

"Some brittle sticks of thorne & briar
Make me a fire
Close by whose living coal I sit
And glow like it." ROBERT HERRICK
1591-1674

"How well I know what I mean to do
When the long dark autumn evenings come.

I shall be found by the fire, suppose,
O'er a great wise book as beseemeth age.
While the shutters flap as the cross wind blows
And I turn the page, and I turn the page.
Not verse now, only prose." ROBERT BROWNING
1806-61

"...When such a time cometh,
I do retire
Into an old room
Beside a bright fire:
Oh, pile a bright fire!

And there I sit
Reading old things,
Of knights & lorn damsels,
While the wind sings—
Oh, drearily sings.

I never look out
Nor attend to the blast:
For all to be seen
Is the leaves falling fast:
Falling, falling!

But close to the hearth,
Like a cricket sit I,
Reading of summer
And chivalry —
Gallant chivalry!"
EDWARD FITZGERALD 1809-83

THE FIRE SPEAKS :-

Listen! the fire is talking,
Speaking with a murmur.
It sings, hums, croons,
Lulls with a glimmer
a glow and a sparkle.

It is a movie of lights
of flickering flames
cavernous grottoes.

It sinks, then revives
roaring, spitting,
cracking explosively.

It sobers again
into a slumbrous glow
inducing reverie, &
enchants the room,
casts spells of contentment.

It is moody & shrewish,
magical, glamorous,
convivial, capricious,
almost personable, &
human one might say.

It can fade & die
So replenish & feed it.
Feed the fire.

"Devour this Yule log, you voracious consumer!"
"Here's kitchen remnants to keep you going!"
"Here's slack to give you a ruby red glow.
And shiny black diamonds for you to despatch!"
How it responds! THE ROOM GLOWS.

Folk enter & rejoice to see this favoured charmer.
They gather round the welcoming genial hearth
[this rarity & luxury of today]
blessing its beneficence.
& the glamour it imparts.

GRAND TOUR OF SCANDINAVIA — 2 WEEKS JULY AUGUST 1985

HELSINKI. ICE CREAMS ON OBSERVATORY HILL, GLIMPSING OUR BOAT 'SILVIA' BETWEEN TREES.

SKI LIFT

LIFT UP ON TO HARDANGER PLATEAU AT GEILO

THUNDERING, CHARGING, BOOMING, HIGH, TWIN WATER FALLS BY THE SCORE, & MORE, ALL ALONG OUR AFTFORD ROUTE

Dear Frances, [friend & eager companion]
We've had 2 months packed into 2 weeks haven't we? Agree?
How did we do it & survive? Each alert hour appeared
to have consumed several hours, each vivid day to
have occupied several days & each short night of deepest
sleep was a much needed & deserved "barrier between day & day."

I've heard of whistle stop tours & now have had one. For
me it was partly a repeat visit (1951), & no less
choc full of illumination; a harvest of experience.

That tiny note book of mine which was
intended only as a written diary,
for I'm used to a very large sketch book,
got filled to choking point with
crowded scribbled memento drawings
which now prompt many memories :—

FIRST :—
Those superb boats which carried us twice
across the waters of Baltic & through
Kattegat by night with their :—

COMMODIOUS LEISURE ROOMS, MANY;
CAPACIOUS CABINS WITH TWIN BEDS;
PLENTY DRAWERS, SHELVES, CUPBOARDS;
EXTRA HOOKS, 2 KEYS, [2 KEY STABLES!]
WIDE TOILET BAR, WIDE BOWL;
HUGE WALL MIRROR;
MOST EFFICIENT SUCTION W·C!
[1st RATE PLANNING & DESIGN]

& THE SUPERB SMØRGASBORG!
SPREAD ROUND DINING HALL, HOT AS WELL AS COLD.
TAP TANKS OF JUICES, WATER, MILK.

All far too tempting!
I reminded self :—
"ENOUGH IS BETTER THAN A FEAST"
"A little meat best fits a little belly" R. HERRICK

ALSO :—

PRANCING STEED

ABOVE CROWN

TIP TOP OF SPIRE FREDERIKSBORG CASTLE ZEALAND
Raining, so took picnic in vaulted walkway with good view.

TRADITIONAL C16 HOUSE GABLE & C17 OLD TOWN SQ. STOCKHOLM
Sketched awkwardly during storm, thunder & lightning - deluge

GABLE EAVE DRAGON TERMINALS LIKE FLAMES

BUILT ENTIRELY OF WOOD, TREE TRUNK COLUMNS, INTERNAL PAINTINGS & SCULPTURES, DRAGON HEAD TERMINALS CUSTOMARY. WITHIN, IMPRESSIVE, BUT GLOOMY.

BASIC DESIGN OF STAVE CHURCH NORWAY

STATUE

BRONZE AGE THE LUR

& BRONZE, MADE IN SECTIONS FOR EASE IN TRANSPORT, PLAYED IN PAIRS, FOR RITUALS, GIVES MOURNFUL NOTE. Used 3000 yrs ago & now found in peat bogs

I HAD TO DRAW SKROG PRESIDING OVER THE VIEW OF OSLO, HE LOOKED SO TRIUMPHANT! IF NOT SMUG!

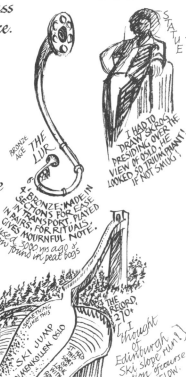

SKI JUMP HOLMENKOLLEN OSLO

SOMETHING LIKE THIS

THE RECORD, 270 + [I thought of Edinburgh Ski slope run!]

Thus is so impressive, we'd love to see it in action of course
LIKE FISH, were the swimmers in the lake below.

Also, those various <u>hotels</u> with their heated bathroom floors, computer keys; [BUT I DID NOT LIKE PASSAGE DOORS OPENING OUTWARDS!] meals of superbly presented smörgåsbord, gourmet foods of infinite variety & enticement, hot as well as cold. I thought of Mr Squeers:- "SUBDUE YOUR APPETITES MY DEARS & YOU'VE CONQUERED HUMAN NATURE";

Those Norwegian <u>trains</u>, which gave such steady comfortable journeys, however curvacious & tunnelled the high mountain passes o[the snowsheds keeping them open the whole winter through.] The <u>Hardanger Plateau</u> gave us glaciers, but no spotting of elk or reindeer.;

Those <u>coach drivers</u>, negotiating such hair pin bends on plunging roads with vertical drops, tunnels, overhangs; ascending over 4,000', descending to sea level along fjords with sheer, colour stained, cliff walls; by turbulent green glacier rivers, WHAT WATER POWER TO SPIN THE TURBINES! waterfalls, double triple; plunging, crashing down in torrents, spouts, veils, cascades, with foam, spray, spume, in thundering roar. VØRINGFOSSEN PLUNGES 600 FT FOR SUMMER TOURISTS! DIVERTED FOR WINTER POWER;

Those <u>sails</u>, past countless quiet islands of holiday homes into <u>STOCKHOLM</u> & <u>HELSINKI</u> harbours; & the long 60 ml grand approach to the head of <u>Oslo</u> fjord, looking towards the high ridges which surround this capital city of <u>OSLO</u>, & passing Akershus Fortress & Bygdöy museums;

Those <u>fruit orchards</u> fitted between mountain side & fjord with peaches, apples, pears & crimson-scarlet cherries [SAME LATITUDE AS SHETLAND 60°];

Those billowing <u>wild flowers</u> starring the waysides of VOSS & GEILO whose country airs scented the beginning & end of our holiday;

Those well chosen, exclusive, daily alfresco <u>picnic spots</u> of ours, which gave such entertaining spectacles;

All these, & many others have richly expanded our horizons, whetting the appetite for yet more,

& NO ROOM TO TRANSFER FROM MY NOTE BOOK THE SPIRES OF KRONBERG'S HELSINGOR, HILLEROD'S FREDERIKSBORG; OR THE FORMAL CHARM OF THE AMALIENBORG, COPENHAGEN; OR THE GORGE OF ODDA, INDUSTRIAL CENTRE, ELECTRICAL PLANT, ALUMINIUM (BAUXITE) IN NORWAY.

SOME SPIRES OF COPENHAGEN, LOW, FLAT, JOLLY, CAPITAL CITY.

Jewelled scale here.

ALLURING ROSENBORG CASTLE SPIRES. We took a picnic in its ROSE GARDEN between showers.

CHRISTIANSBORG PALACE SPIRE, WITH 3 CROWNS. Here we donned slippers for the fine floors.

COPPER SPIRAL STAIRWAY OUR SAVIOUR'S CHURCH. I climbed 400 steps onto the spiral; but too windy to reach the golden ball. Green & gold

4 DRAGON SPIRE STOCK EXCHANGE! Christian IV's idea. He helped twist the dragon tails!

RIDDARHOLM CHURCH PANTHEON

Swivel chairs, illuminated alarm clock; TV; radio; fridge BUT NO TEASMAID OR KETTLE!

TWO SPIRES OF STOCKHOLM'S OLD TOWN, & TOP KNOT CHARM.

Really needed binoculars for these

LOVELY, UNIQUE, LACY, SIMPLE STATEMENT IN WROUGHT IRON ARCHES. SPIRAL STAIR THRILLING TO EXAMINE

GERMAN CHURCH SPIRE PROJECTING WINGED FIGURES VISUALLY EXCITING

WHAT ARCHITECTS! & STEEPLEJACKS!

SUCH MOTOR ROAD ENGINEERING! NORWAY. Like a burrowing snake

ONE OF 4 OXEN PULLING PLOUGH. "GEFION FOUNTAIN" [WIZARD PYTHON ESCONCED BELOW] WATER SPRAYS FROM NOSTRILS.

A most ugly statuary group

I thought of D.H. Lawrence's poem ...."A snake came to my water trough On a hot hot day...."

HANS ANDERSEN STATUE CITY SQ COPENHAGEN

TWIN BEARS CITY HALL COPENHAGEN

CHERRY TREES Polythene tents for the fruit by the fjords of Hardanger

IN STROGET COPENHAGEN POST CARD TROLLEYS ON WHEELS very popular

A JOLLY ARRAY OF MARKERS ON FISHING BOATS. DRAGOR COPENHAGEN.

??? REMEMBER THE GUITAR MUSIC IN THE ROCK CHURCH, HELSINKI? WHAT ACOUSTICS!

Remember that violent storm? STOCKHOLM;
Old Town Sq. full of folk. Suddenly they vanished.
Rain pelted. Torrents swept the square. Lightning split
the heavens. Deafening thunder rent the air, exploding,
raging, bellowing. Quite my worst storm ever.
Pressed against historic porch under
Hanseatic gable, we chatted to a fair haired
local young wife, with great hilarity;
REMEMBER:-
the 2 lively Finnish sisters,
piloting themselves round Europe?

the jolly, talkative Chinese boy
who couldn't afford the Round Tower?

the 7' Dane who walked us criss cross
to St. Olaf's, very informative chap;

the Swedish student on Stockholm's high
Observatory Hill, mad on computers;

the Norwegian cyclists who asked
us to direct them; much laughter;

the tree trunk acrobatics of those
two red squirrels at Geilo?

the swinging River Suspension Bdge, Voss?
ALL SMALL INCIDENTS BUT A
LIVELY PART OF THE HOLIDAY CANVAS.

Being myself mad on sculpture, I inspected
the small scattered modern ones in Stockholm's
Humlegården. Later was again carried away by
Carl Milles Gdn on its S-facing cliff setting above the
water, the ethereal figures flying against snowy clouds,
dappled with leafy tree shadows, or splashed with fountain jets.

In Oslo, Gustav Vigeland's extraordinary outpouring
astonished; such fertility of invention! Being once a
sculptor, I was interested that he first modelled life size
in clay, then from plaster casts his team of masons carved
his granite family groups. I enjoyed too the lively bridge figures;

The Viking ships in Oslo must be recorded for their
grace, beauty of form, perfection in design – a joy to the eyes – &
so impressively displayed in the white vaulted chambers
with pulpit galleries, built specially to house them.

Also must be recorded the Geilo Hotel's exceptional
collection of furnishings, textiles, decor, various, tasteful;
AND the exemplary quality & presentation of foods there.
' EAT ALWAIES SO THAT THOU STILL HAVE AN APPETITE.'
ie · STOP WHEN YOU FEEL LIKE JUST A LITTLE MORE!

ONE OF A PAIR OF SWANS OF 'FOUNTAIN' CITY HALL, OSLO.

WEDGE SHAPED, PURPOSE BUILT TENTLIKE HOME FOR 'FRAM' THE VESSEL WHICH TOOK NANSEN & AMUNDSEN, FARTHER N & S THAN ANY PREVIOUS SHIP. Inside, this museum is huge & light, & the 'FRAM' exciting to explore.

'Black Swans' to me

A TRIO OF VIKING SHIPS @ @ THE 'OSBERG', THE 'GOKSTAD' & THE 'TUNE.' I couldn't stop drawing them from every angle trying to catch the subtle beauty & grace of these three shallow draught vessels, quickly manoeuverable in wide open seas.

IN OSLO MUSEUMS BYGDØY

MOTIF, MOSAIC FLOOR, MILLES MUSEUM

"ORPHEUS CALLS UP THE SPIRITS" BY CARL MILLES CONCERT HALL STOCKHOLM. NOBEL PRIZES ARE AWARDED HERE. We took our picnics on the steps!

PEGASUS A TRULY MARVELLOUS SCULPTURE by CARL MILLES seen against sky, on its mast

14" SOME JOLLY HIP HIGH SCULPTURES IN HUMLEGÅRDEN, STOCKHOLM.

NO SPACE TO SQUEEZE IN DROTTINGHOLM PALACE, ITS FOUNTAINS, PARTERRES & CHINESE STYLE [TRIANON] RETREAT.

KON TIKI BALSA RAFT 1947
ON 9 BALSA LOGS & BAMBOO DECK THOR HEYERDAHL + 5 CROSSED PACIFIC 4,300 MLS. PERU TO POLYNESIA, drifting on the S Equatorial current, in OSLO, BYGDØY MUSEUM

FACSIMILE EGYPTIAN PAPYRUS REED BOAT RA II ATLANTIC CROSSED 1969 HEYERDAHL, A DARING, ENTERPRISING, INVESTIGATOR. I was rooted drawing this from every angle.

TRAINING SHIPS, OSLO HARBOUR

TO REACH THE OSLO BOAT MUSEUMS, TAKE THIS FREQUENT, CHEAP, FERRY ACROSS TO BYGDØY "MUSEUM PENINSULA" 10 mins of breezy appeal.

2 RUNNING FIGURES IN AN EXPLOSION OF JOY. BRONZE. BY VIGELAND. Very infectious CHEERY!

ALL LIFE SIZE Intimacy here FIGURES IN CONVERSE

MOTHER & SON WITH PROBLEM? HUMAN SITUATIONS CARVED IN GRANITE GUSTAVE VIGELAND OSLO.

Markets everywhere are unfailingly magnetic, & that of Helsinki on the harbour above sparkling water, with such an abundance of colour in flowers & fruit was the summit of charm, as 28 yrs ago. But I missed the craft stalls of before.... Did we arrive too late for these?

Helsinki's Civic Sq

is very special, don't you think ? up on a slope towards the sea & crowned by the high domed Cathedral nobly set on its lofty platform & approached by that broad flight of 36 ? steps.

I thought of other historic SQUARES abroad:- Venice, Salamanca, Winter Palace, Red Sq., Samarkand, Marrakech, Madrid, St Peter's etc; EACH DISTINGUISHED, EACH FLAT.

John Keats wrote:-
"Nothing ever becomes real until it is experienced"
I felt this among the deepest fjords. Geographic magnificence, awesome, primeval, Nature's preponderance over man [Wordsworth says it all]
I sensed the same forces in N. Zealand.

It's how the imagination interprets what one sees that can make an experience such a fascinating thing, I always think

As you see, Frances, I've crammed 4 limiting pages with just a few of our many experiences among such amicable folk.

It was good to meet Delys again after 30 yrs & Harold her husband; then there were:- Ernie & Laura, Joann & Molly, Ronnie & Kay, Peggy & Iretta, Stuart & Ina, John & Helen, Chris & Eleanor, Lenn & Shirley, Maureen & Mum, Douglas & Dorothy, & many other friendly souls among the VERY FRIENDLY SCANDINAVIANS.

How the hassle of life can blot away these memories if we don't hoard them.

With all the best wishes to you both, from &

COPENHAGEN

STORK & BULRUSH. STROGET. FOUNTAIN · COPENHAGEN

Tivoli Gardens & fountains were a delight. Those bubble columns 4-5' fascinated me.

COPENHAGEN ROUND TOWER

SLOPING SPIRAL BRICK RAMP CLIMBS THROUGH 9 'STOREYS' THEN 59 STEPS TO THE GALLERY! Peter G. drove up in horse drawn carriage!

Violent storm STOCKHOLM

Thoughts of Norse Myths; of STRINDBERG, of IBSEN, BJORNSON, NOBEL, LINNAEUS, coloured our days, & refrains from Greig & Sibelius echoed.----

LUGGAGE. WHAT A CHORE!

"Wedding Carriage" Motif from a woven wall panel. BARDOLA HOTEL Geilo, was an Aladdin's cave of 'objets d'arts.'

MAVIS AMANDA FOUNTAIN, HELSINKI.

A memory of the CATHEDRAL, HELSINKI, raised high on its platform.

BEVY OF NORWEGIAN PEDAL CYCLISTS. Scandinavia consumes icecream by the ton! [& PEACHES]

Our best of all good picnics, on rocks 2,000' above Geilo's river opposite ski runs.

In the Swedish train, us, circumspect, others haphazard!

These students scattering world wide.

Thoughts too of the HANSEATIC League of Merchants who controlled trade in the Baltic & other ports (13 onwards).

To SYRACUSE, 1955.

FISHERMEN sort their lines in a series of rings, spread across the wide harbour terrace right under our window. Free entertainmt.

HEATH ROW to MILAN April 2. [Us two + 28 various.

Barley sugars & ear plugs sent round, & off we go!]

Alps stunning! Tiers of snowy peaks, blue sky. Look down! There's the Rhone twist, Montigny! There's Lausanne! that's Montreux! See the railway at Brigue! That's Chateau D'Oex! Drifts of narcissi there; a pity we can't exactly see them!

PAPYRUS OF ARETHUSA'S FOUNTAIN

Graceful slender PAPYRUS grows by the Ciane Anapo River, & among the white ducks in the charming SPRING OF ARETHUSA. Pindar & Virgil have both sung the praises of this spring. Pietro washed his jacket in the sacred waters of the Cyane.

Milan to SYRACUSE, train. 27¼ hrs, & compartment to ourselves from Rome 900mls for £3.30. What value for money! the ferry across the Straits, by Scylla-Charybdis all inclusive!

After Naples we woke to geranium hedges; judas trees; fig trees; olives, vines, lemons, wild gladioli, & children who balanced jars upon their heads.
THE WHOLE TRAIN RAN ON TO THE FERRY AT MESSINA

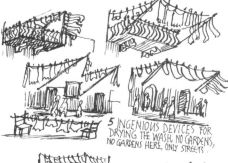
I went out before breakfast to see this flotilla of ships arrive in port. Sails furled, they docked to unload cargo.

ROPE MAKER at dock side. Caïques discharge cargoes of building materials for new SYRACUSE, & bare footed labourers transport bags of cement. NO CRANES!

From the train to NOTO we plunged down into the countryside, mapless, thro' orange groves to the river for our picnic. Tadpoles—'big as whales' said M, were basking in the shallows & young frogs leaping from among the reeds. I was in heaven.

Peasants gathered round with gifts:- 12 lemons, beans, orange blossom, gladioli.

Away down river a big washing was progressing in stages:-
① Wash the week's dirties, & spread out to sun dry.
② Wash household linen
③ Shed your own clothes & don the sweet sundried ones.
④ Wash today's set.
⑤ Return home spotless!
SOME 20 PEASANTS THUS ENGAGED!

5 INGENIOUS DEVICES FOR DRYING THE WASH, NO GARDENS, NO GARDENS HERE, ONLY STREETS

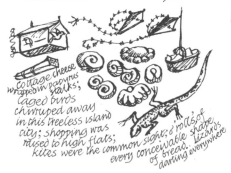
Cottage cheese wrapped in papyrus stalks; caged birds chirruped away in this treeless island city; shopping was raised to high flats; kites were the common sight; & rolls of every conceivable shape of bread. Lizards darting everywhere

We fell deeply in love with Ortygia [quail] the Old SYRACUSE, also with the Noto countryside. Invigorating scented air wafting from orange blossom, fast flowing rivers, [good as Scottish burns, not turgid with glacier water like Swiss ones, & we found few in Greece, just dried river channels,] & in Syracuse, harbours, quays, boats, fisher folk, cheap ferries ½°, history, Greek Remains, Roman Remains, friendly helpful people, scenes of great beauty all around. We'd have been happy to stay longer. M's 'Blue Guide' was invaluable.
MY SKETCH BK IS LYRICAL & A JOY TO PERUSE, PAGE BY PAGE

WE HAD THIS DEAR LITTLE ROOF FLAT ABOVE THE HOTEL FOR 5 NIGHTS. OH, JOY!

LIMESTONE QUARRIES WHERE 7000 ATHENIANS STARVED TO DEATH

LATOMIA OF CAPPUCCINI- CHAMBERS, COLUMNS, ARCHES, CAVERNS, & NOW A STAGE MOST INGENIOUS.

FISHING BOATS, GAILY PAINTED BEAR A PROJECTING RAM OR BEAK, & ON EITHER SIDE OF THE PROW, THE PROTECTIVE EYE & ANCHOR SIGNS STRONGLY DEPICTED.

Contd on p. 60, 'SICILY.'

FLANDERS

Dear Peggy,

When are we going to take this projected trip to <u>Amsterdam</u>? Late Autumn is the best time I'm sure. It will be my fourth visit, yet I long to see again those lively brush strokes & most moving Van Gogh paintings, the Rembrandts with such evocative mystery, & those patrician town houses ranged with such period distinction along concentric canals. WE SHOULD ALSO TRY TO GET TO THE KROLLER MUHLER MUSEUM AT ZUTPHEN.

I remember looking down on the city by moonlight back in 1935, flying home from Russia & wondering how our great plane (30 on board) would find foothold among this network of moon reflecting canals & polders.

<u>Sept 1952</u>, <u>a flight to Amsterdam</u>, & train on to Mme Verhoeven's kind hospitality in <u>BRUSSELS</u>, for the World Fair, she lived opposite the Entrance. We used her top flat, so had front seats above this spectacular festival.

BRUSSELS

I gasped at the facades of the <u>GRANDE PLACE</u>. Was there ever such an array of sculptured facades & gilded C17 pilasters? & now along came bands, banners, bells, & floats of the <u>Fruit Festival</u>. Men on stilts, effigy figures carried high above the crowds, flags flying, song, dance, clogs, a galaxy of colour. Later on, Mary, stopping to post a letter uttered a sharp squeal. "A wasp," thought I, "lumbago?" No. A pigeon having enormous relief from a parapet above!! SHE THEN ADMITTED SHE'D BEEN TREATED TO THIS IGNOMINY IN BOTH VENICE & MILAN! MAGNETIC ATTRACTION?

<u>Sept 1965</u>. <u>Harwich to The Hook</u>, for a further look at Amsterdam, was a convenient crossing from Bishop Stortford where I worked. Then we went to THE HAGUE [HEDGE] to see the Vermeers & Rembrandts in Mauritshuis & the Geemente moderns.

<u>June 1966</u>, <u>Leith to Rotterdam</u> was equally easy from Haddington E·LOTHIAN, for a North Sea crossing in celebration of retirement. Driving on, after a steady sail, we were able to take a look at the Polders (and dykes) of great fertility. What a feat of 1920 engineering! Lelystad commemorates Dr Lely

"No plough stands still when a man dies" WE WERE REMINDED LOOKING AT "FALL OF ICARUS" BREUGHEL.

"DID YOU SEE WINDMILLS? & CLOGS? & PEOPLE WEARING CLOGS?" asked Kay. We did, & had large juicy pears & grapes after our omelette for breakfast. VERY HOT SULTRY WEATHER SEPT 1952

WHAT GABLES! VARIETY! MERCHANTS (17 HOUSES TREE BORDERED QUAYS ON CANALS, BRIDGES VARIOUS. WE WALKED FIGURES OF EIGHT. TERBORCH MUSIC LESSONS THEN. CONCERTGEBUOW NOW.

MAID SERVANT VERMEER

AMSTERDAM

BRUSSELS GRAND PLACE · VERY TALL NARROW FACADES, HIGHLY DECORATIVE :- Sculptured figures, split pediments, pinnacles, consoles, pendentives, pilasters, balustrades. Very rich & exciting.

TWO SLIGHT BUT HAPPY MEMORIES OF A LUCKY VISIT TO ST PETER'S ABBEY IN GHENT JUST BEFORE CLOSING. MEDIEVAL PAINTING, SCULPTURE, STAINED GLASS, DISPLAYED WITH GREAT ARTISTRY.

NORTH SEA

NETHERLANDS

THE HAGUE · UTRECHT · ROTTERDAM · HOOK · UTRECHT

CALAIS · BOULOGNE · FRANCE · OSTENDE · BRUGES · GENT · ANTWERP · BELGIUM · BRUSSELS · LEUVEN

GRASLEI SKYLINE GHENT '52

1952, BRUGES enchanted. The Rly Stn seemed to be set in a green park, grass, trees, flowers, (NOT SO TODAY.) A lace maker sat engrossed at her cushion. We wandered along by the Minnewater & Swannery, revelling in the magical charm. The Beguinage, so set apart, & so period, one felt to be intruding on past ages. Carillons, canals, back waters, bridges, towers, churches, civic squares, quiet retreats, all have an aura which puts Bruges in a class of its own. A dream city if ever there was one.

1985. What must be noted of this ART TOUR by 'PROSPECT.'? First & foremost our gesticulating lively Guide Claire, who instructed us so knowledgeably, kept us on the alert, and cared for her brood like a mother hen.

The Art Galleries! How we gloated in BRUGES over the works of Memlinc, Van Eyck, & David, Van der Weyden, discriminating over small details with keenest interest. The Casket of St Ursula captured. Each painting we felt to be an aesthetic meal.

Van Eyck's "Mystic Lamb" took us to GENT for an early viewing of this astonishing and exquisite masterpiece, & the BRUSSELS Museum showed a fine collection of Breughel's paintings & many others.

In ANTWERP CATHEDRAL, paintings of Rubens & his house nearby were of gt interest, a town mansion of real distinction.

LOUVAIN. Such steep roofs & pinnacles! The quiet dignity of 'LAST SUPPER' by Dirk Bouts in the Cathedral; the brick buildings pink with cream stone dressings of the Beguinage backwater; were all impressive & memorable.

A 'lightning whistle stop' tour it was, an appetite whetter! And so good to meet like minded people, birds of one feather; Dellie & Ian McI from Shincliffe, Hugh & Helen F of Banbury, & other like enthusiasts, & SUCH PLEASURE TO BE ACCOMPANIED BY EDNA G.
   THANK YOU, Peggy for all yr interest in my travels, & for yr good neighbourliness. BEST WISHES, DorisAnn.

SKYLINE FIGURES, CITY SQUARES

ANTWERP
IN DEN VOS 1699 BRUSSELS
BRUGES DE GOUDEN MEERMIN BRUGES
HOTEL LE PANIER D'OR BRUGES
ANTWERP
ANTWERP

BRUSSELS' LACE MAGICAL

Initial pins
Spangle bobbins
continuous threads
Filaments
fibres
All the tools of the trade
filigree, net, web, mesh, knotting, interweaving, what intricacy! what exquisite effects.

LACEMAKER

COURT YARD SCENES BY P. DE HOOCH & DOORWAY VISTAS ACROSS CANALS, made me curious to peep through open doors, looking for an echo of those homely tiles doorways & figures of his genre pigs.

METSU
THESE PAGES OUR YOUNG MEN ALSO WEAR LONG HAIR

THE YAWNER BREUGHEL

GHENT
ST. BAVON CATHEDRAL, WHERE STANDS THE GREAT VAN EYCK ALTAR PIECE, 'THE MYSTIC LAMB.' ON THE GRASLEI WATER FRONT; I TOOK PICNIC, Mᵉ BOUGHT MAC.

PINNACLES, TURRETS LACE LIKE GALLERIES, ROOFS PRECIPITOUS. AT LEUVEN

BRUGES
OUR TWILIGHT EVENING PICNIC HERE WAS MAGICAL. ACROSS THIS MINNEWATER BRIDGE, LIE THE BEGUINAGE PRECINCTS.

ISTANBUL 1951

WITH NIGHT THROWN IN AT ROME!

Two days of flying, 4 stops, & a night in Rome is B.E.A's 1951 schedule for getting us two from London to Istanbul.

via Nice, over Corsican mountains, into Rome for Maundy Thursday, churches seething with people & lights, but St Peter's closed, black cat again! Good night in Hotel BEA. GOOD FRIDAY gales, alarming turbulence approaching Athens. Nearly collided with Parnassus!

Above Istanbul we zoomed around for ½ hr, [M.M.B. stiff with anxiety!] *& landed thro' thick grey cloud.* Then we two British & 9 others were herded into waiting room for the customs call, separately, by name. "GOODCHILD" was bawled first & 3 surly officials enquired :- "Jewellery?" NONE! Incredible! "BURNETT" next. Then smiles all round, & off we went in taxi to our high room PERA with skyline view of graceful mosques & minarets, & Roman Viaduct of OLD STAMBOUL ranged above the Golden Horn— SUPER!

WE HAD ARRIVED.
PRAISE BE !

A GUILTY YET HAPPY SKETCH SCRIBBLED ON KNEE BUT SURELY A TRAVESTY

THE BLUE MOSQUE

of SULTAN AHMED [our favourite] is the only one outside MECCA having six minarets. Each bears 3 lace like galleries from which the messarin voice calls the faithful to worship 5 times daily. The presence of foreigners is no longer resented, so on our 2nd visit we donned slippers & dared to sit, & sketch or write & gaze.

An executive arrives, replaces his trilby with skull cap, drops umbrella & prostrates himself repeatedly.
A worker appears, with brazier under his arm, & prostrates.
A beggar enters, piles his rags on the carpet & washes his feet arms, head at a trickle emerging from pillar base!

MOSQUES

What tracery of colour!!! Arabesque tiles line walls up to the high dome, ringed with light.
A sea of rich oriental rugs large & small, carmine coral russet, tawny, lie cheek by jowl on top of rush mats spread over the uneven spacious floor.
Feel their softness with your stockinged feet, as your eyes gloat, & your ears note the murmured intoning of Moslems who squat/kneel at their prayers.
At the Muezzin's call to prayer, men leave their market below, & wash feet head hands at courtyd fountains before entering.

MOSLEM AT PRAYER TABLE

YENI CAMI MOSQUE STANDS BY THE WATER 2 MINARETS

SULTAN AHMET MOSQUE SIX MINARETS UP ON HILL

Mosques stand out along the high points of OLD STAMBOUL. SLOPES down to the Golden Horn are thick with a jostle of buildings. Boats jostle too on this busy stretch of historic water.

Nosing our way thro a maze of bewildering streets & markets we got lost. This concerned Potter left his stance to put us on our way

This cheerful lady, brushing PRAYER RUG in her window longed to exercise her English. "I know" "I know you are BRITISH, You are so beautiful." Ha, ha!

Today, 1951, the religion of Islam is no longer the state religion. Turkey is now a modern secular republic & every religion is free. No books were printed in Arabic after 1929. The Fez & Veil abandoned under K. Ataturk

The SERAGLIO, Palace of the Sultans, TOPKAPI, was an experience apart. Such a setting, high above the Sea of Marmora! Views to the Princes Isles, across to Scutari, up the Bosphorus, & over Galata Bridge along the Golden Horn to the skyline with Roman Viaduct & Mosques, which add such a fairylike charm to the view.

About 30 Pavilions are spaced out across comely gardens. Each is distinctive in style;– A WHOLE GAMUT OF FLAVOURS, ORIENTAL TO FRENCH RENAISSANCE! & each given over to displays:– plate, jewels, textiles, china, furniture etc & Arabic Calligraphy – oh! how entrancing! What a magical feast!

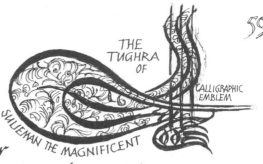

THE TUGHRA OF SULIEMAN THE MAGNIFICENT

CALLIGRAPHIC EMBLEM

BEYOGLU PERA GALATA
GOLDEN HORN
BOSPHORUS
SCUTARI
OLD STANBOUL
PALACE
PRINCES ISLES
SEA OF MARMORA

GALATA. A STEEP RISE FROM THE WATER UP TO THE OLD WATCH TOWER.

We saw a carrier transporting 20 wooden chairs up this steep hill. BEGGARS? YES, POVERTY & SQUALOR.

Our Sunday 2 hr sail along the Bosphorous had one, just one alarming incident. At the terminus, my precious sketch book was confiscated by a jackbooted armed uniformed official, & we two were set under guard. Now, the only 2 passengers on board, we realised our mistake. We had sailed into the military area beyond the submarine boom, & should have alighted at the penultimate stop with other passengers. Oh dear! ONE HOUR'S CONFINEMENT before the engines revved for the return journey when my innocence won back the sketch book. RELIEF! HOW I DREW MY HORNS IN, & POCKETED THE PRECIOUS BOOK!

PEDLARS bring the task of carrying to a fine art
GRAIN? BEANS?
WATER?
A CREEL OF JERUSALEM ARTICHOKES SKILFULLY ARRANGED
HOT DRINKS?

Oriental rugs are our weakness. Could we buy one from our meagre funds? The Grand Bazaar was a maze of cavernous tunnels rising up hill & dropping, dark & spooky. We gave up the search preferring to bargain in open air markets, where every thing from sulphur to fried livers, ultramarine to kebabs are sold.

OFF OUT TO BREAKFAST IN BEYOGLU ONE MORNING TO JOIN JANET C. BEFORE SHE WENT TO WORK.

OFF FOR THE DAY WITH HIS COOKIES

These hamals are resting before taking the long stretch of Galata pontoon bridge – said to be "the most wonderful pathway in Europe". They are fitted with head pads & back harnesses, & can carry staggering loads & weights.

IN BEYOGLU MARKET UNDER TREES

MY PENCIL AT ONCE BROUGHT AN AUDIENCE

ISLAND OF SICILY

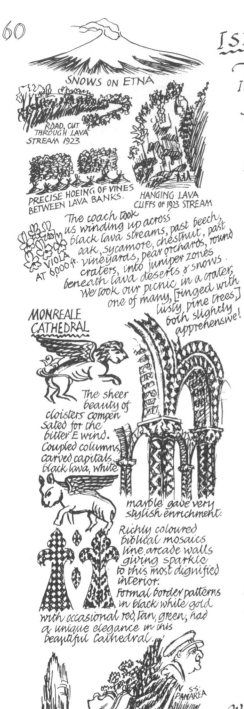

SNOWS ON ETNA

ROAD, CUT THROUGH LAVA STREAM 1923

PRECISE HOEING OF VINES BETWEEN LAVA BANKS.

HANGING LAVA CLIFFS OF 1923 STREAM

VIOLA AT 6,000 ft.

MONREALE CATHEDRAL

The sheer beauty of cloisters compensated for the bitter E wind. Coupled columns carved capitals, black lava, white marble gave very stylish enrichment.

Richly coloured biblical mosaics line arcade walls giving sparkle to this most dignified interior. Formal border patterns in black white gold with occasional red, tan, green, had a unique elegance in this beautiful Cathedral.

IN S.S. PANAREA

THE FARAGLIONI OBELISK BEYOND, & PUMICE CAVERNS, LAVA STRIATIONS, AS WE SAILED THE COAST OF LIPARI beloved of geologists & seismologists, but to me more than a trifle spooky!

BEAUTIFUL **TAORMINA** next, by train. It was too popular for us, but from it we took the Grand Tour of Etna— singular & of great interest in every way.

The coach took us winding up across black lava streams, past beech, oak, sycamore, chestnut, past vineyards, pear orchards, round craters, into juniper zones beneath lava deserts & snows. We took our picnic in a crater, one of many, [ringed with lusty pine trees,] both slightly apprehensive!

Then local bus to **MESSINA**, & night train [to save hotel bill] via **CEFALU** to **PALERMO** where M's purse was pinched, & where we found ourselves locked in a Monastery Garden for 4 whole hrs! We explored Monte Pellegrino & Capo Zafferano above Conca d'Oro. The local bus took us [bottoms nipped!] to MONREALE, thrilling.

A coach trip westerly showed us **SEGESTA TEMPLE** remote among hills; **TRAPANI** salt pans, **MARSALA**, **SELINUNTE**, & home by train. My great sensation was Mt **ERYX** village perched on its high rock in a mist of fairytale dream, beyond belief.

Surely Sicily has everything we decided, as whim took us here & there across the island by local bus, train, coach. Wild mtn scenery of the interior, dramatic views to the sea, Greek history & mythology from C7 B.C. Archimedes! very good coastal fertility etc NEVER A DULL MOMENT!

AEOLIAN SEA

TYRRENIAN SEA

ITALY

SICILY

ERYX SEGESTA PALERMO CEFALU TAORMINA TRAPANI MARSALA SELINUNTE AGRIGENTO SYRACUSE NOTO

MEDITERRANEAN SEA

CAPPELLA PALATINA, PALERMO, most special; exceptionally remarkable.

FROM TAORMINA the bus took us up the winding road, & groaned its way to the peak of CASTEL MOLA. Later we sprinted down on the old road, now a mule track, & found our way up to Taormina castle for a good view of the steep track we'd taken.

CASTEL MOLA

THE TOOTH

A FEW MOTIFS FROM THE DECORATED CARTS. THE WHOLE CART IS PAINTED, RIGHT DOWN TO WHEELS & SPOKES. BROAD SIDES HAVE PAINTINGS OF THE PALADINS. FINIALS, BRACKETS ETC ARE CARVED.

I sketch away Easter Monday while MMB studied Blue Guide.

This is an approximate memory sketch. Will this cranky old bus climb this steep precipitous road? How can folk live isolated on this rock 2460' up? LEGS DANGLING OVER CLIFF FACE, WE TOOK A PICNIC IN SEA MIST, THEN CROSSED PATTERNED FLAGSTONES TO THE LITTLE PUBLIC PARK. VENUS APHRODITE'S SEAT WAS HERE.

ERICE

The Temples of **AGRIGENTO**, superbly sited were to me less exciting than ERICE, which captured me.

STROMBOLICCHIO

STROMBOLI

YES! STROMBOLI IS INHABITED! White cube houses above black beaches; palms, figs, olives, vines along coast, 2 domed churches with bell towers, & much tunny fishing & STUDENTS INTERNATIONAL

We two, the only ladies sailing from Sicily to **Naples** across the **Aegean**, [in a boat smaller than our Hebridean ones,] received V.I.P treatment during our 2 nights & one day on board, (33 hrs) liquers, petit fours between meals, pampered with blankets against the gusty Aeolis wind, visited by captain, crew, German Biologist, & Dutch Geologist etc. We called at about 10 island ports, row boats coming out to us, the last Stromboli. [no fireworks here!] Arrived Naples 6.0 a.m. breakfast on beach [picnic,] & STRAIGHTWAY JOIN C.I.T. FOR SORRENTO, AMALFI, POSITANO, POMPEII, lovely tour. MY SKETCH BOOK IS LIVELY WITH DETAILS.

CENTRAL SPAIN 1985

FELIPE IV
1621-1665
PLAZA ORIENTE
PALACIO REAL

SCULPTURED
DAY DREAMING IDEALIST
DON QUIXOTE, & COMPANION
LIFE LOVING SANCHO PANZA
UNDER OLIVES & ABOVE POOL
PLAZA DE ESPAÑA.

Vaguely I had visualised the high rolling
plains of Old Castile crossed by rocky
ranges & Sierra de Guadarrama.
Vaguely I thought of Conquistadors; the
Inquisition; the Armada; Bull fights; Guernica.

I thought of the Romance of Spain; of Cervantes, Lope de Vega, Columbus; of Velasquez
El Greco, Goya; of Palaces, Processions, Fiestas, Flamenco; of tortilla, gazpacho,
paella, (BUT LATE DINING,!) & then last of the Prado, Segovia, Toledo, & these won me over!

I burned with desire to see SEGOVIA'S Roman Aqueduct; TOLEDO rising steeply from the
encircling R Tagus; EL ESCORIAL in its austerity; & the bastioned walls of AVILA etc.

These cities of the high central plateau, scorched in summer, bleak in winter,
drew me. We chose March & early April, & had brilliant sunny days.

HIGHEST CAPITAL MADRID IN EUROPE 2,200'

In 1969 my friend MMB piloted me on a daybreak tour of OLD MADRID.
Trafficless streets. The world was ours save for a few early risers:-
Puerta del Sol, alleys, lanes, churches (many) San Iáro Cathedral,
peering here, gazing there, fascinated by ceramic name plates,
Plaza de la Villa, Plaza Mayor, where we took a needy breakfast
after exploring its 8 arched entrances.

GOLD JEWELLED VOTIVE CROWN, EXQUISITE.

FAR TOO SHORT WAS THIS MORNING'S VISIT TO THE MUSEO ARQUEOLOGICO

DAMA OFRENDANDO UN VASO—STONE

LA DAME DE ELCHE

LAS CUEVAS, [THE ROBIN HOOD OF CASTILE] TAVERN SIGN

CURTAIN TASSELS, KNOCKERS, DOOR STUDS 'N' FREQUENT EVIDENCE.

TWIN CLOCK TOWERS PLAZA MAYOR

VELASQUEZ 1599 1660

GOYA 1746 1828

EL GRECO '541 1614

HERMITAGE OF THE VIRGEN DEL PUERTO. E.O.G VERY PATIENT FOR MY SKETCH.

CALLE DE SAN MARTIN   CALLE DE CORDON
ARRESTING JOLLY DESIGNS FOR STREET NAMES, OLD MADRID.

The 1985 visit gave salute to many previous 'friends':-
The PRADO & ARCHEOLOGICAL MUSEUMS specially delighted;
The PALACIO REAL, a visual feast; chandeliers! clocks!
Mus. de SOROLLA & its paved garden charmed; & so on.

E.O.G. & I, full of zest, sped from place to place, on
winged feet, appetites whetted for more & still
more. Squares, parks gardens gave repose & picnics.

CRYSTAL PALACE RETIRO PARK

REMINDED OF HOME!

EXHIBITION HALL LIGHT, GRACEFUL, UPLIFTING;

THE RETIRO,
CAMPO DEL MORO,
ROSALES etc

Traffic? Yes, one expects
this in a Capital. But oh,
oh, the fumes! AND WHAT'S
HAPPENED TO DEL SOL'S FOUNTAIN?
AND I MISSED SOME BOULEVARD TREES!

BETIRO PARK ALFONSO XII

THESE ARE NOT FOR ME!

REQUIRED:- A GOOD PAIR OF FEET, WELL SHOD. WE CERTAINLY HAD THEM.

SEGOVIA

"All a wonder & a wild desire" R.Bg

We crossed the snowy Sierra de Guadarrama & stopped at the high Pass [toboggans, chair lifts skis & skiers] to see 'The frolic architecture of the snow' W.R.W. Emerson

Invigorating air sent us climbing up among the scented pines.

THE SNOWY PASO DE NAVACERRADE.

Motifs from caps

THE STRUCTURAL SIMPLICITY DELIGHTED

OUTSIDE SEGOVIA, IS LA VERA CRUZ CHURCH (13 KNIGHTS TEMPLAR, A LITTLE GEM OF INTRINSIC BEAUTY. [REMINDS OF HOLY SEPULCHRE, JERUSALEM.]

This golden city, compact & rising steeply, piled above the fork of its 2 rivers, the Cathedral dominating all, immediately worked its spell.

Climb, climb, for its Alcazar is dramatically perched, a lofty fairy tale palace, a fortress, perched on an eagle promontory, its many sharp spires pricking the sky.*

Climb again. The Cathedral sports a host of needling pinnacles, consistently encircling its 3 storeyed chevet, beautiful to behold, but the interior locked against our entry.

Churches numerous; arcaded outer cloisters, fine bell towers, & how I wanted to stop & draw the sculptures, loitering within & without. "What's round this corner? & up that cobbled lane? A museum? a market? a tavern? a view?" the short hours flew.

But for me the greatest wonder of all was that mighty Roman Aqueduct striding the valley on giant legs. What a pigmy one feels gazing upward, awed & amazed.

THE ROMANTIC LOOKING ALCAZAR ethereal & sylphlike from without, a robust fortress within; Royal Chambers, Chapel, prison etc. Black knots of clinker spot the patterned walls.

Clinker buttons on white walls

SAN MARTIN

MY SEAT IN PLAZA

Column figures! Sculptured caps! I gloried in them. So much to peruse & enjoy inside & outside

Mountain snows beyond the towers, spires, domes.

THE BULK OF SEGOVIA CATHEDRAL seen beyond trees of its PLAZA

3276'

For rapture, see SEGOVIA in evening light.

SKETCHED GATEWAY IN LOFTY WALLS AS WE DROVE THRO'

I was transfixed before these towering, mighty arches; felt puny, insignificant. MONSTER GRANITE BLOCKS, NO MORTAR, NO CLAMPS, HELD BY THEIR OWN WEIGHT. COUNTLESS ARCHES (1 AD. I wanted to kneel in respectful homage "we petty men steal under his huge legs..."

Used as film scenarios

STREET CROWNED LAMP

PALACE LAMPS

THE PALACE OF *EL ESCORIAL* HAS ALWAYS MYSTIFIED ME. Now, this, my [limited] visit, has elucidated much of Philip II's Royal Seat, Monastery & Pantheon. The rare, priceless Manuscripts & Missals riveted me, & the 32 marble caskets of crypt, astonish'd.

FROM ONE PONDEROUS EDIFICE SET UPON THE MOUNTAIN SIDE, TO ANOTHER SITED WITHIN → THE MOUNTAIN SIDE:- THE LONG CRYPT LIKE MEMORIAL TO CIVIL WAR FALLEN 1936-39 →

Siesta? No! Rest? No! Coming to Escorial? YES! Siesta? No!

What a library! A gold mine of treasures! Take your lens! Codex Aureus etc
I am a doodler myself

THE CROSS STANDS AT 4570' A LIFT INSIDE

What a conception! some walls de nuda phantasma make you think

THE CROSS 500' HIGH

The long crypt tunnels 5 ml into rock where the Basilica blasted directly under the Cross. Monastery too. Valhalla! Gen Franco lies here too. Terrace whence the town & the

GRACIAS, EL ESCORIAL, ADIOS!

TOLEDO,

El Greco's adopted Imperial city. I was all agog. Ever since seeing his dramatic painting of it under storm, I've longed to set foot here in Toledo, piled as it is on bare rock, reaching skywards high above the encircling R. Tagus, boxed in by climbing fortress walls, & crowned by the Cathedral.

"THE TRENCHANT STEEL TOLEDO 'TRUSTY' S. BUTLER 1660

TOLEDO

THE ROCK OF TOLEDO RISES ABOVE THE R. TAGUS, WHICH LOOPS ROUND LIKE A MOAT.

The exclusive view across to this soaring city excels, so no wonder El Greco was moved to paint it. From the river steep roads & alleys, tiers of honey coloured houses, pink roofs, & a sky line of belfry towers from S. Juan de los Reyes via the Cathedral to the block of the Alcazar.

GATEWAYS into the city? Yes. Impressive fortress-like structures they are. BRIDGES crossing the Tagus? I counted 3 ancient [gated] & one of recent time.

PLAZAS? The urban Zocodover has its market, & from smaller squares lead tangles of alleyways. Don't get lost in this very intricate network! Explore, & lose yr way again! Mansions, studded doors, grilled windows, walls of stone panels set in brickwork, most eyecatching. What an array of colourful patterned plates, & here's a craftsman of damascened jewellery with tiny hammer tap tapping in those fine gold threads. Here you're on cobbles, here on ceramic tiles. Look down, look up, but don't miss the local folk!

SLENDER HEADS, GESTICULATING HANDS; EL GRECO 1541-1614

PUENTE DE ALCANTARA
MUDEJAR TOWER W 1484
BAROQUE GATEWAY E. 1721

A CHIMNEY!

DOOR KNOCKER
SPOUT END

ARCADED TOWER, & TILED ROOFS, ABOVE GARDEN OF EL GRECO HOUSE.

The Cathedral absorbed a whole morning. What a combination of artistry rich with craftsmanship:- Choir a wealth of carving; High altar all sculpture; Chapels, grilles, railings & the Monstrance silver gilt (16; the Cloisters; triple crowned spire; but the baroque Transparente was not for me.

El Greco's house, its cloister court, its garden; I revelled in them. His trial palette was revealed under a hinged frame in Talavera Hospital, & What gargoyles in Juan los Reyes! One could NEVER exhaust such a museum city.

BE SURE TO SPEND A NIGHT OR TWO - OR MORE FOR EVENING SUNSET STROLLS - & MORNING SUNRISES, PERHAPS.

TRIPLE CROWNED STEEPLE & PINNACLES & FINE TOWER CATHEDRAL

PUERTA DE ISAGRA 'NEW' GATEWAY
REPLACING THE OLD MUDEJAR GATE

WHAT IMPRESSIVE GATEWAYS TO DRIVE THROUGH!

PUERTA DEL SOL MUDEJAR style
ERECTED BY THE HOSPITALLERS (14

226 MASTER MASONS GAVE THE DAZZLING BEAUTY HERE.
SEEN BETWEEN DARK CYPRESSES THE GLEAMING WHITE STONEWORK OF SAN JUAN DE LOS REYES. 1476

WHAT GARGOYLES!

"TOWERS ARE FOR GOING UP, CORNERS FOR GOING ROUND" SAID AVRIL

The Palace of ARANJUEZ on the Tagus, classical, baroque & full of Bourbon splendour. Tapestries, Pompeian ceilings, Ballroom, Smoking Chamber [Alhambra Palace] etc, & the China Room horror of porcelain plaques. Avenues of English elms & planes & famous gardens surround the Palace, parterre, pools, cascades etc but no chance to see the Royal 'Cottage' with R Maria Louise luxurious dressing room.

THE PALACE OF LA GRANJA [7 mls from Segovia] WE DID NOT VISIT, NOR EL PARDO.

Our good companions, so enthusiastic:- Sandy, Eva & Muriel, Dennis & Myrtle, Kathie & Rachel, Neal & David, Rhoda, Avril, & sons, from Dundee University, & Angela.

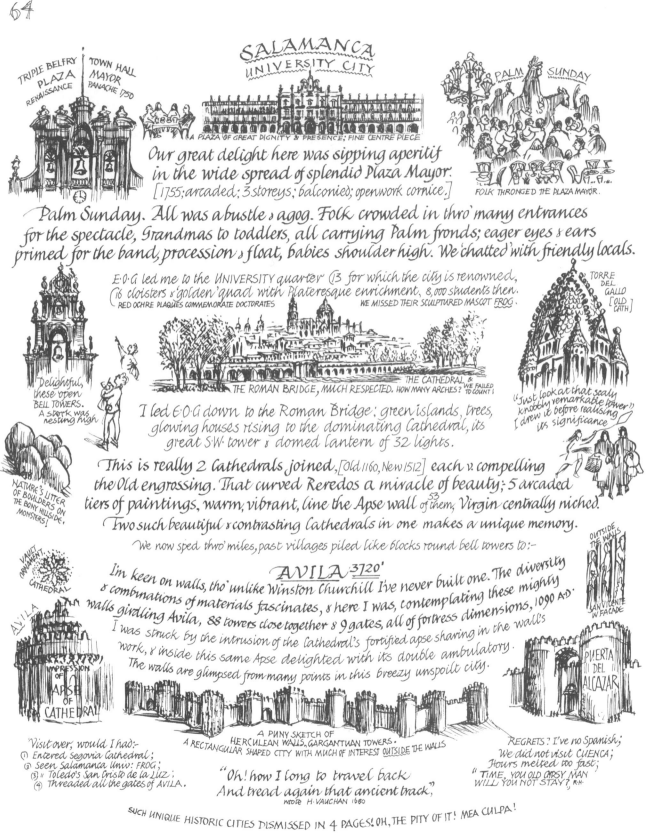

SALAMANCA
UNIVERSITY CITY

TRIPLE BELFRY PLAZA RENAISSANCE · TOWN HALL MAYOR PANACHE 1750

PALM SUNDAY

A PLAZA OF GREAT DIGNITY & PRESENCE; FINE CENTRE PIECE

FOLK THRONGED THE PLAZA MAYOR.

Our great delight here was sipping aperitif in the wide spread of splendid Plaza Mayor. [1755; arcaded; 3 storeys; balconied; openwork cornice.]

Palm Sunday. All was a bustle & agog. Folk crowded in thro' many entrances for the spectacle, Grandmas to toddlers, all carrying Palm fronds; eager eyes & ears primed for the band, procession & float, babies shoulder high. We 'chatted' with friendly locals.

E·O·G led me to the UNIVERSITY quarter (13 for which the city is renowned, (16 cloisters & 'golden' quad with Plateresque enrichment, 8,000 students then. RED OCHRE PLAQUES COMMEMORATE DOCTORATES · WE MISSED THEIR SCULPTURED MASCOT FROG

TORRE DEL GALLO [OLD CATH]

Delightful, these open BELL TOWERS. A stork was nesting high

THE ROMAN BRIDGE, MUCH RESPECTED. HOW MANY ARCHES? WE FAILED TO COUNT!

THE CATHEDRAL, &

"Just look at that scaly knobbly remarkable tower" I drew it before realising its significance

I led E·O·G down to the Roman Bridge: green islands, trees, glowing houses rising to the dominating Cathedral, its great S.W. tower & domed lantern of 32 lights.

NATURE'S LITTER OF BOULDERS ON THE BONY HILLSIDE, MONSTERS!

This is really 2 Cathedrals joined, [Old 1160, New 1512] each v. compelling the Old engrossing. That curved Reredos a miracle of beauty; 5 arcaded tiers of paintings, warm, vibrant, line the Apse wall of them, Virgin centrally niched. 53

Two such beautiful & contrasting Cathedrals in one makes a unique memory.

We now sped thro' miles, past villages piled like blocks round bell towers to:-

VAULT ORNAMENT. CATHEDRAL.

OUTSIDE THE WALLS

SAN VICENTE W FAÇADE

AVILA 3720'

I'm keen on walls, tho' unlike Winston Churchill I've never built one. The diversity & combinations of materials fascinates, & here I was, contemplating these mighty walls girdling Avila, 88 towers close together & 9 gates, all of fortress dimensions, 1090 A·D.

I was struck by the intrusion of the Cathedral's fortified apse sharing in the wall's work, & inside this same Apse delighted with its double ambulatory.

The walls are glimpsed from many points in this breezy unspoilt city.

AVILA

IMPRESSION OF APSE OF CATHEDRAL

PUERTA DEL ALCAZAR

A PUNY SKETCH OF HERCULEAN WALLS, GARGANTUAN TOWERS. A RECTANGULAR SHAPED CITY WITH MUCH OF INTEREST OUTSIDE THE WALLS

Visit over, would I had:-
① Entered Segovia Cathedral;
② Seen Salamanca Univ: FROG;
③ " Toledo's San Cristo de la Luz;
④ Threaded all the gates of AVILA.

"Oh! how I long to travel back And tread again that ancient track," WROTE H. VAUGHAN 1680

REGRETS? I've no Spanish; We did not visit CUENCA; Hours melted too fast; " TIME, YOU OLD GIPSY MAN WILL YOU NOT STAY? R·H·

SUCH UNIQUE HISTORIC CITIES DISMISSED IN 4 PAGES! OH, THE PITY OF IT! MEA CULPA!

MOROCCO
A FEW NOTES
ON THE WING
& FROM THE SIDELINES

YELLOW TASSELS
MIMOSA RAMPANT

HAS HE A CHARMED LIFE, THIS
SNAKE CHARMER WITH TAMBOUR?

"You spotted snakes with double tongue"
"The snake throws her enamell'd skin"
I RECALLED FROM W.S's MID's DREAM

PSALM 104:
"For fir trees
are a dwelling,
for the storks."
BUT HERE, BEING SACRED BIRDS,
THEY GRACE ROOFTOPS & TURRETS.

Dear M & F, SALAAM. Peace be unto you,
& blessings on you for the gentle push
you gave, which propelled us to
this land; a world so apart,
that the visit now lies
like an elusive dream, a
mirage, a wraith, which
must be anchored & knitted into
the present lest it fade away.

ESSENTIAL
TO ALL
PEASANT
FAMILIES &
MARKETEERS
IS
THIS
HUMBLE
TRANSPORTER
THE
UBIQUITOUS
LADEN
DONKEY MADE ME
RECALL LINES FROM CHESTERTON & DE LA MARE:
"There was a shout about my ears,
And palms about my feet." GKC
& POOR OLD 'NICHOLAS NYE', DE LA MARE

DISDAINFUL?
ARROGANT?
POMPOUS?
HAUGHTY?
REFERENCES:- John Baptist's
"Raiment of camel's hair",
"Camel & needle's eye",
"Strain at a gnat,
swallow a camel",
& R.K's "cameelious hump."
I RECALLED BIBLICAL

So libraries here & there,
books by the score, & art galleries,
are helping to pin down, &
illuminate, a hoard of gains.

What a thing retirement is
to give such opportunities for
timeless pause & browsings,
thus entrenching & extending
the kaleidoscope of holiday scenes.

BRITISH MUSEUM MANUSCRIPTS DELIGHTED,
VICT & ALBERT MOORISH EXHIBITS THRILLED.
OH! THAT PRICELESS ARDABIL CARPET!

ENORMOUS HOODS TO THE ARAB
'DJELLABA' WITH TASSEL
BEHIND

VEILED
CITIZEN
SHOWING KOHL
EYES ONLY [PRAPS NOSE TOO]
& COUNTRY TRADER IN
HUGE BRIMMED REED HAT,
HEAD SHAWL, & RED CANDY-
STRIPED SKIRT,
LOAD ON
BACK
& IN EACH HAND

MY SMALL
POCKET SKETCH
PADS WERE EVER
"AT THE READY"
& MOSTLY IN
FULL USE.

OUR
ONE OF
GUIDES

WALLS OF MARRAKESH

[*Islamic Art, in its wide ranging fields, holds endless fascination for us. Museum displays in Morocco & back here beget thirst for more & more.*]

Impacts from our visit are legion;- the friendly people; unhurried figures of robed men; stately veiled women; little girls with babies swaddled to their backs; playful little boys with laughing black button eyes; tents; country fairs; donkeys; camels; storks; mosques; door knockers; & specially:-

HASSAN TOWER RABAT
ON ITS HIGH PLATFORM DO CLIMB IT FOR THE VIEW; SEA, RIVER, SALE, CHELLA. [BRICK BUILT]

"SONG OF SOLOMON IV 16

WALLS; mighty ramparts, formidable in height; of fortress dimensions. They climb slopes, corner outcrops, rise tier upon tier; circle the Medinas, secure kasbah fortresses, surround tombs. Walls of the oasis of Marrakesh, as you may remember, stretch palm fringed for miles around, on the high level sunbaked plain; 500 Tantallon castles would not make up the length!

ABDUL AHMED
OUR 2 SCHOOL BOY GUIDES IN FEZ MEDINA, ENTHUSIASTS, EAGER, KINDLY, WELL WORTH THEIR HIRE.

GATES, set within the barbaric splendour of these walls; single double or triple horse shoe arched; carved, battlemented, may be richly tiled & inlaid.

CHELLA
BRICK BUILT
GATEWAY POWERFULLY DISTINCTIVE, JUST OUTSIDE RABAT, LEADS TO A RAMBLING GARDEN, MAGICAL, OVERGROWN, TIMELESS, WITH ROMAN RUINS, MERINID TOMBS, SACRED POOLS, & RIVER BELOW; A PLACE TO MUSE IN, I THOUGHT.

WARM GREETING

MEDINAS, [the walled ancient towns] are a labyrinth of narrow alleys which climb drop, twist, divide; a medieval warren bewitching bewildering. The panniers of a laden donkey can pin you to the walls.

"DYED IN THE WOOL" RAINBOW PENDANT HANKS DRAPE DYERS' ALLEYS LIKE BANNERS & BUNTINGS

TASSEL FRINGED HAT OF WATER SELLER, WHOSE THEATRICAL DECORATIVE COSTUME HUNG WITH BELL & SILVER COINS & DRINKING BOWLS, KEPT ALL CAMERAS BUSY; HOLDS THE WATER

A GOAT SKIN CARRIED ON HIS BACK

Look out! here's a tall laden mule descending on us. A yell from the muleteer is lost among the calls & cries, footfalls clatter & hubbub. You have yet to visit FEZ for this climactic experience.

DYE VATS BY THE SCORE; & DYED SKINS

BY THE HUNDRED, ARE SPREAD ON TANNERY ROOFS TO DRY

SHOPS are tiny booths crammed with goods which pen the owner in on all sides. To escape, he must crawl under or swing out over the goods on a suspended rope!

BABIES TOSS ABOUT ON THE BACKS OF PLAYFUL CHILDREN; A SMOOTHER RIDE WITH MUM.

"AWAKE O NORTH WIND; COME THOU SOUTH; & BLOW UPON MY GARDEN, THAT THE SPICES THEREOF MAY FLOW OUT."

THE LIDDED POTTERY
TAJEEN
IT WILL COOK TO PERFECTION THE COUS COUS BASED MEAT CHICKEN VEGETABLE & HERB NATIONAL SAVOURY DISH
& FISH OF COURSE!

VERY SMALL GLASSES OF MINT & HERB TEA WERE SERVED & SIPPED [STEAMING HOT] AS WE INSPECTED CARPETS, OR SUN BATHED BY ROOF OR GARDEN POOLS.

SNIFF! what a fragrance! Is it herbs? mint? aloes? musk? wych hazel? or the burning of incense? Now what a stench! You certainly need a nosegay visiting the TANNERS' quarters!

WE HAD A MINT SPRIG

A pause to sip the customary steaming mint tea is most welcome & refreshing.

How good it was to meet & make friends with Pat & Cyril Kent of Thornton Rust, WENSLEYDALE

RABAT, FEZ, MEKNES, MARRAKESH, TANGIER, TETOUAN, CHECHAOUEN & OTHER TOWNS, ALL HAVE THEIR MEDINAS & THRONGING MARKETS, WITH PEOPLE JOVIAL, EAGER & FRIENDLY.

EXPECT TO BARGAIN, SO DON'T ACCEPT STARTING PRICE.

CORIANDER SAFFRON SPICES, V. CHEAP. HAND HELD SCALES.

The <u>SOUKS</u> [markets] sprout wares. They spawn on the ceilings, pack walls by dozens & spill on to pavements in a plethora of goods, chattles & artifacts;— tooled leather; incised copper; carpets; black art magic; charms; potions; spices; henna; hoofs, etc. Discs of pastry & bread, fed into charcoal ovens, fruits both fresh & dried; vegetables galore very beautifully presented; & there could be up to a mile of assorted pottery ware arrayed along the roadside.

Craftsmen at work in tiny lock-up booths sit X legged on small platforms hammering, stitching away, pleased to have spectators. We gazed in fascination. Nimble fingered boys stand in narrow alleys twisting threads for tailors & tassel makers. What rainbow colours come from the dyers vats, & what an array of skins, spread on roofs, come from the tanneries!

From all this busy hubbub the mosques & medersas were a cool shadowed retreat with courts, arcades fountains & minarets. Cadences of the muezzins' call to prayer drifted away above the clamour.

But the <u>PEOPLE</u>! They were my chief attraction! Towns women, veil'd, stately in the long tailored djellaba, their country cousins mysterious in the voluminous white haik, patriarchal men in the long striped hooded burnous, or cool white pantaloons. "WAS THAT ABRAHAM?" "IS THIS MOSES?" we queried. Were we pestered by guides & touts? Yes! indeed. But 2 alert 14 yr olds piloted us safely thro the warren of FEZ.

When you go to the fine capital of <u>RABAT</u>, be sure to climb Hassan Tower for the view. [double walls with ramp as in Giralda of Seville] The spacious high platform at its foot, sprouts rows of columns giving children a unique playground.

Be sure to visit also the hillside site of <u>CHELLA</u>; its huge gateway; haunting groves; moss covered ruins; exotic gardens, & its sacred eels.

Crossing the fertile, rolling green coastal plains, "This land is rich; flowing with milk & honey" I thought.

TAKE REST. A FIELD THAT HAS RESTED, GIVES A GOOD CROP.

FROM SCHOOLS WAFTED THE CHILDREN'S CHANTING OF THE KORAN.

A SERIES OF OCTAGONAL LAMPS FEZ

KARAOUINE MOSQUE FEZ

PLAIN WHITE WALLS HAVE FOCAL POINTS IN THEIR EMBOSSED & FIGURED HEAVY BRONZE DOORS; BOLD KNOCKERS; HINGES; CARVED DOOR HEADS; WINDOW SHUTTERS; & LAMPS. FINE CRAFTSMANSHIP SCARCELY COMPLIMENTED BY THESE DRAWINGS.

"AND THERE WE SIT IN PEACEFUL CALM QUIETLY SWEATING PALM TO PALM." A. HUXLEY

IN RABAT

GILT & AZZURO

THIS GIVES AN IMPRESSION OF THE 8 PILLAR ORNAMENTS APPROACHING MOHAMMED V MAUSOLEUM

IN MARRAKESH THESE SIMPLE STEPPED & INSCRIBED MARBLE FLOOR SLABS DEEPLY IMPRESSED ME; FLOOR TOMBS IN THE BEAUTIFUL ISLAMIC MAUSOLEUM OF THE SAADIANS.

MEN'S YELLOW LEATHER BABOUCHE

STRAW SUNSHADE HAT OF COUNTRY FOLK, BROAD BRIM ANCHORED WITH BLACK CORDS & BOBBLES ABOVE RED STRIPED HAIK WRAP. TOWN SHOPPER, WITH VEIL WEARS TAILORED JELLABA

1 DIRHAM = 10p approx

LONG STRINGS & ENDLESS DISPLAYS OF POTTERY. SELECTION A PROBLEM, BARGAINING FUN!

MOORISH TEXT AGAINST HEAT:— NEVER DO IN THE SUN THAT WHICH CAN BE DONE IN THE SHADE. NEVER STAND WHEN YOU CAN SIT, NEVER SIT WHEN YOU CAN LIE, NEVER RUN WHEN YOU CAN WALK. TAKE INDOOR SHELTER FROM SCORCHING SUN

Luscious oranges [two a penny!] stone fruits, threaded figs, vegetables, fish, cereals, poultry, cattle, minerals, forests, make it self supporting.

Nearing the High Atlas were the humped contours of the semi desert, ochreous tan & gold; farms like fortresses; & then snow capped peaks 13,664' against blue sky. We drove into a steep green valley with rushing river [& paddled] The mighty rock walls rose almost sheer to the snows. Terraced brown hamlets perched here & there. Peasants worked the fertile floor. We later passed the Ski Resort of IFRANE 5000', pitched roofs, very Swiss in style.

Then to MARRAKECH. You loved it I know, & I'll never forget① the Koutoubia Minaret; ② the Saadian Tomb Pavilions opening from a garden, the walls richly carved, lofty coffered vaults above the simple carved & inscribed marble slabs; ③ the huge magnetic Square, throbbing with life, agog with entertainers; snake charmers, glass eaters, acrobats, story tellers, drummers, quack doctors, charms, potions, fortune tellers, etc each encircled by an eager, goggle eyed crowd.

The huddled, fascinating old University town of FEZ, truly oriental, is in a class of its own. It defies précis description, & must be seen to be believed.

A short visit to MEKNES suggested a city once splendid, historically barbaric, with a network of walls of defence. The wool market held me; mountains! of fleeces, piles of wool, hanks, rollocks, scales suspended from trees, country folk sitting, standing, bargaining.

We fitted in a breezy walk up thro' the Roman ruins of VOLUBILIS, lingering by the quite unprotected mosaics, & saw the sacred white town MOULAY IDRISS set on the dark hillside beyond.

Limited time for this tour inclined us towards visual indigestion, but in retirement one can chew the cud.

This short letter is but a précis of some of our many impressions.
With best wishes from
DorisAnn G.

— margin notes —

THE FLOWERING STEM OF THE AGAVE OVER 20'. GROWS FROM HEDGE LIKE A LOFTY TELEGRAPH POLE.

[THE RED EARTH GILDED WITH MARIGOLDS...]

JOLLY OCHRE TENT IN MEKNES, STRIPED & PATTERNED IN BLACK.

KOUTOUBIA MOSQUE, MARRAKESH. OUR VIEW APPROACHING IT.

ROMAN MOSAICS VOLUBILIS

"SULTAN WITH HIS POMP. SULTAN AFTER, ABODE HIS DESTINED HOUR & WENT HIS WAY." EDWARD FITZGERALD

ANOTHER LOVELY MOORISH INTERIOR.

WHITE HILL TOWN OF MOULAY IDRISS [FATHER OF FEZ] SEEN ACROSS VALLEY OF PINE, THUYA, FIR, JUNIPER, CYPRESS, AS WE STOOD AMONG RUINS OF VOLUBILIS.

"THY WATERS, ARE THEY WHITE HONEY, OR SILVER?" ASKS THE POET.

WASH BEFORE PRAYER. IN A MOSQUE COURTYARD. "'TIS THE HOUR OF PRAYER". G. BYRON. "LATE & EARLY, PRAY". H.W. MOSQUES ARE NOT OPEN TO THE PUBLIC.

MINT & GREENERY BASKET TALL AS HIMSELF

FEZ HAS 50 SPRINGS + RIVER.

THE SOUK RECALLED:- "MANNA & DATES IN ARGOSY TRANSFER'D FROM FEZ." JOHN KEATS

FIGS ARE THREADED ON LOOPED OR DANGLING STRINGS

BAB BOU JELOUD, ONE OF MANY ENTRANCES TO THE MEDINA, FEZ.

ONLY EYES, KOHL OUTLINED, ARE VISIBLE.

BAB MANSOUR, THE GRANDIOSE GATEWAY OF MEKNES

REMEMBER 16 MLS OF RAMPARTS & ARCADED CAVALRY STABLES

THE SAVAGE, BRUTAL HUMAN MONSTER, MOULAY ISMAEL, HOBNOBBED WITH LOUIS XIV

THE ENVELOPING WHITE HAIK

LOADED WITH WOOL

" While breathlessly you're being hurled
By plane & train right round the World,
We hope you'll have good health, good fun
Then happy homing when its done !! "

SO RHYMED B·E·B TO ENCLOSE
WITH HER FAREWELL BUTTONHOLES.

"I'll put a girdle round about the earth
In forty minutes," said Puck; but we took longer'!

Our 'World' Tour

Thus we entitled it in fun,
knowing full well our travels were far from global
& would skip infinitely more of this world
than was included.

"East, West, Home's best," they say.

But the homes of those abroad
have great attraction too.

And I take leave to misquote:-
'What should they know of Britain who only Britain know?'

In 1950, two friends were planning their world tour:
"That is something I'll never achieve," I regretfully thought.

Yet in 1969 it became a reality in spite of the strict £50
Foreign Travel Allowance imposed for that year.
How could we manage the costs? Friends & relatives en route
would come to us for reciprocal visits, & thus ease our finances.

1969 🌿 OUR VARIOUS GOODBYE BUTTON HOLES 🌸🍂

A chance remark to a chance concert acquaintance gave me my first visit to NEW YORK in 1969. In the Interval, Joyce said to me, "My husband is located in MANHATTAN for a spell. I return there shortly. Please do come & visit us in our flat."

A most enticing idea. BUT HOW? Problem:- £50 only, was the total abroad Travel Allowance for 1969; & we'd already planned to visit in Spain [see Record in 'GLIMPSES OF CITIES' 1984] Resourcefully we conjured and contrived thus:- A gift of £50 to Joyce's daughter [a quid pro quo]; for PORT ARTHUR friends, £200 deposited here; ditto for NEW ZEALAND friends; exchange holidays arranged for friends in TORONTO, BANFF, VANCOUVER, SEATTLE, AUCKLAND, TASMANIA, CANBERRA, SYDNEY. All travel tickets, car hire, etc bought here in advance. THUS ALL WAS SETTLED. Q.E.D. Hurrah!

DETAILED PREPARATION BEGAN. I SET TO WORK & MADE:-

5 sets of folded drawing paper sewn into book form; one separate cardboard cover to hold them, & a hand/shoulder satchel with biro slots, to carry same.

Now the wardrobe. Light weight luggage essential, ∴ dual/triple purpose clothes. Frigid temps in the Rockies, torrid temps in Fiji, ∴ natural fibres desirable. NO NYLON. Shops were combed for jolly silks & cottons, also for feather weight woollens. The 1969 fashion for short shifts, very convenient! The sewing machine took all cloths thin, thick, or tough, with equal good humour, & turned out jackets skirts, dresses, beach gear etc holdall bags, purses etc in good style. Total luggage weight, 28 lbs
THUS, NO PORTERS, NO BAGGAGE TROLLEYS REQᴰ.

Harrods produced light weight blue Shetland tweed for raglan jacket & wrap round skirt, [this doubled for extra bed cover]; & various woollens also.
SEAM & POCKETS IN BOTH

7 OZS
6 POCKETS
4 OZS
Loose, lightweight slip on s. pink quilted nylon jacket
Silk dressing gown; 3 ozs
voile beach dress 2¾ ozs
interchangeable

Twill silk dress 2¾ ozs
& bolero jacket 2½ ozs

JOHN LEWIS provided charming figured sea island cottons silks, voiles in fashionable psychedelic colours.

SHORTIE NIGHTIE 2 OZS
TWO OF THESE

Twill silk from DUNFERMLINE MILLS, so cheap, 5/- yd, that I dared to dye it double for sleeveless dress & sleeveless coat, used with voile blouses
4 OZS
3.5 OZS
4 OZS
DOUBLE SILK
DOUBLE SILK LINING

BEACH TOP, WRAP ROUND BEACH SKIRT, BOTH IN DOUBLE JAP SILK

FISH BONE SEW TIE, & NIPPER PEGGING, were the favoured methods.

THE 'X' COUNTRY MOORLAND 'SHORT CUT' TO PRESTWICK AIR PORT, VIA MAUCHLINE VIEW POINT, WAS BARRED BY ASTONISHED CATTLE!

WHAT HOODOOS, WHAT FATES LAY IN WAIT? High jacks? Strikes? Cancellations? Engine failures? Riots? Road blocks? Hold ups? Stampedes? And what about dysentery? mosquito bites? sharks? snakes? jelly fish stings? Wolves & bears we could avoid! FOR GUARANTEE we insured against everything.
"OUT OF THIS NETTLE, DANGER, WE PLUCK THIS FLOWER, SAFETY" we quoted; & "FAINT HEART NEVER WON FAIR LADY!"

SO PLANS WERE FORMULATED, then revised adapted, bis. Letters sped in all directions with enquiries, requests, dates. Libraries were ransacked; Atlases thumbed, maps scrutinised; Time Tables juggled with; Documents, Currencies procured.
"NOTHING VENTURE NOTHING WIN" we said & "COURAGE MOUNTETH WITH OCCASION".

A LONG-POSTPONED RETIREMENT JAUNT THIS; BUT NOW AT LAST, OFF WE GO ON OUR WELL EARNED SPREE, WITH FEATHER WEIGHT LUGGAGE BAGS

TWO OF THESE BARELY 12 OZS IN WEIGHT BLACK & LINED
ZIP HOLDALL. IN BLACK YACHT NYLON, linen reinforced. Belt handles, 12 ozs. Made before today's light travel bags appeared.

4 OZS
HAND BAG. white nylon lined silk, reinforced. NYLON PURSES, NOTE CASES for various currencies.

2 OZS
SKETCHING SATCHEL white reinforced nylon. Belt handles, shoulder strap. 6 biro pockets.

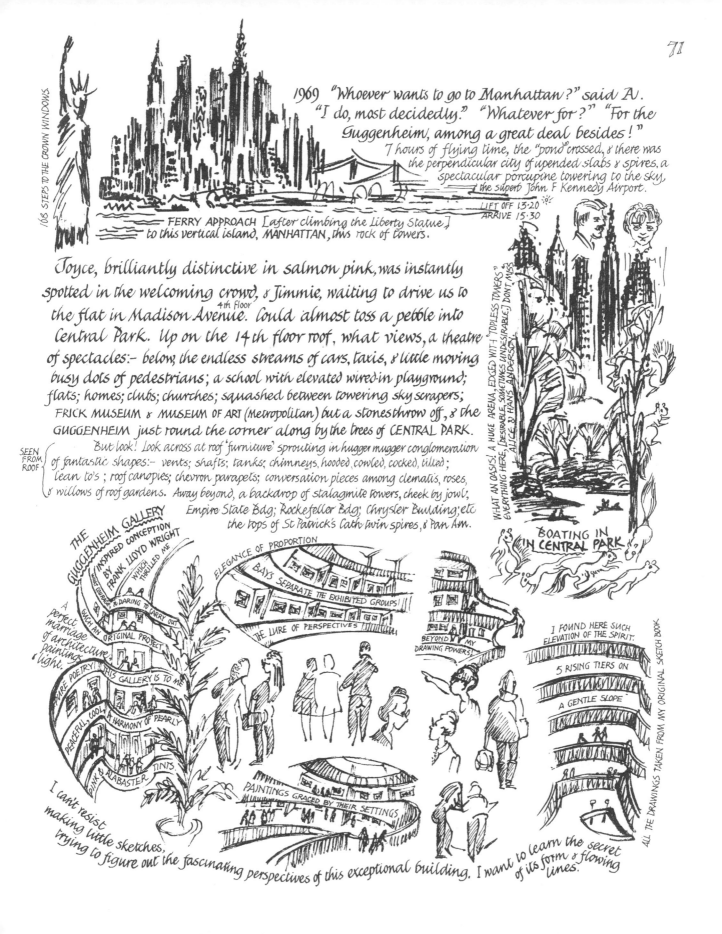

168 STEPS TO THE CROWN WINDOWS.

1969 "Whoever wants to go to Manhattan?" said A. "I do, most decidedly." "Whatever for?" "For the Guggenheim, among a great deal besides!"

7 hours of flying time, the "pond" crossed, & there was the perpendicular city of upended slabs & spires, a spectacular porcupine towering to the sky, the superb John F Kennedy Airport.

LIFT OFF 13·20
ARRIVE 15·30

FERRY APPROACH [after climbing the Liberty Statue] to this vertical island, MANHATTAN, this rock of towers.

Joyce, brilliantly distinctive in salmon pink, was instantly spotted in the welcoming crowd, & Jimmie, waiting to drive us to the flat in Madison Avenue. 4th floor Could almost toss a pebble into Central Park. Up on the 14th floor roof, what views, a theatre of spectacles:- below, the endless streams of cars, taxis, & little moving busy dots of pedestrians; a school with elevated wired-in playground; flats; homes; clubs; churches; squashed between towering sky scrapers; FRICK MUSEUM & MUSEUM OF ART (Metropolitan) but a stonesthrow off, & the GUGGENHEIM just round the corner along by the trees of CENTRAL PARK.

SEEN FROM ROOF

But look! Look across at roof 'furniture' sprouting in hugger mugger conglomeration of fantastic shapes:- vents; shafts; tanks; chimneys, hooded, cowled, cocked, tilted; lean to's; roof canopies; chevron parapets; conversation pieces among clematis, roses, & willows of roof gardens. Away beyond, a backdrop of stalagmite towers, cheek by jowl; Empire State Bdg; Rockefeller Bdg; Chrysler Building; etc the tops of St Patrick's Cath twin spires, & Pan Am.

WHAT AN OASIS! A HUGE ARENA, EDGED WITH "TOPLESS TOWERS" EVERYTHING HERE, [DESIRABLE, SOMETIMES UNDESIRABLE.] DON'T MISS ALICE & HANS ANDERSON.

BOATING IN IN CENTRAL PARK

THE GUGGENHEIM GALLERY INSPIRED CONCEPTION BY FRANK LLOYD WRIGHT WHICH THRILLED ME

A perfect "marriage" of architecture, painting, light.

WHAT COURAGE & DARING TO CARRY OUT SUCH AN ORIGINAL PROJECT

PURE POETRY THIS GALLERY IS TO ME

PEACEFUL, COOL, A HARMONY OF PEARLY PINK & ALABASTER TINTS.

ELEGANCE OF PROPORTION

BAYS SEPARATE THE EXHIBITED GROUPS!

THE LURE OF PERSPECTIVES

BEYOND MY DRAWING POWERS!

I FOUND HERE SUCH ELEVATION OF THE SPIRIT.

5 RISING TIERS ON

A GENTLE SLOPE

ALL THE DRAWINGS TAKEN FROM MY ORIGINAL SKETCH BOOK

PAINTINGS GRACED BY THEIR SETTINGS

I can't resist making little sketches, trying to figure out the fascinating perspectives of this exceptional building. I want to learn the secret of its form & flowing lines.

MIXTER-MAXTER PAGES, GIVING A MERE FLAVOUR: A HOTCH-POTCH, SHOWING JUST A FEW MANHATTAN DRAWINGS

OCTOBER 5-11 1969 IN 3 PAGES.

Invigorating, these lively sculptures of the fountain pool next the Buffet, inside extensive, vast MET. MUSEUM OF ART, by CENTRAL PARK.

We supped ice creams here for an interval in our peregrinations.

A pause while viewing the HUNTINGTON HARTFORD COLLECTION, GALLERY OF MOD ART. GOMA

Then an evening concert, Philharmonic Hall.

ARCADED STREET WALK, CULTURAL CENTRE G.O.M.A 1964, (see above)

IN HENRY FRICK'S (19 STATELY COLUMNED RESIDENCE. now a MUSEUM of distinction

TERRACED GARDEN OF MODERN ART

After a knickerbocker glory, Joyce knitted away while I drew in the terraced Sculpture Garden of M.O.M.A, MUSEUM OF MODERN ART.

FROM THE TOP OF EMPIRE STATE BUILDING 1931, [1472'] TOWERING WITH 80 mls VISIBILITY ON A CLEAR DAY, OURS WAS MISTY. I GAZED DOWN ON TO THE BEEHIVES OF THIS TEEMING CITY, A CLOSE-PACKED WILDERNESS

OF PILLARS, PRISMS, BLOCKS, OBELISKS, CLIFFS CANYONS, [BINOCS IN HAND] SEARCHING THE CROWDED TOWERSCAPE TO PICK OUT VIGNETTES OF FLOWERING ROOF GARDENS, SUN BATHERS, SWIM POOLS, HELI-PADS, HOUSES, HOMES. THIS VIEWPOINT IS A VISITORS 'MUST'

I recalled Walt Whitman: "I stood as on some mighty eagle's beak,"
& Andrew Young's 'missel Thrush seeing folk:- "crawl at the bottom of the air,"
William Cowper's "Higher than the heights above Deeper than the depths beneath,"
& London's Monument; & Eiffel Tower, & mountain peaks. BUT LOOK! SEEING IS BELIEVING! Snug between the skylarking towers are the trees, homes, mews OF GREENWICH VILLAGE.

DOOR KNOCKER WASHINGTON MEWS

CHARACTERS GARMENT QUARTER

NANNIES, CENTRAL PARK

FOLK IN THE GUGGENHEIM GALLERY

QUEENSBOROUGH BDGE

BROOKLYN BRIDGE

MANHATTAN BRIDGE

Round Manhattan Island we Jaunted by boat; cruising weather, jolly picnic. I counted 17 bridges. MAYOR changing skylines; Gracie Mansion OF N.Y. United Nations; Welfare Island etc. You can also use the Culture Loop Bus, or wing it by helicopter.

LINCOLN CENTRE

N.Y. STATE THEATRE 1966.

MET. OPERA HOUSE 1966

PERFORMING ARTS

Here are 14 acres of walks, trees, patios, sculptures, fountains set between fine impressive modern halls & arcades:- we enjoyed Prince Igor the MET OPERA HSE; 1966 LIBRARY & MUS. OF PERFORMING ARTS 1965, VIV. BEAUMONT THEATRE '65; JUILLIARD SCH OF MUSIC 1968, ALICE TULLY C. HALL we lunched at a deli.

INSIDE THE PHILHARMONIC AVERY FISHER HALL 1962 GLASS WALLS, & OUTSIDE CLOISTERS 1962.

METAL SCULPTURE IN FORECOURT LIBRARY & MUSEUM

I OFTEN, MUCH ENJOYED THESE CLOISTERS TEA IN AUTOMAT, A SIZZLING PIZZA TORTELLINI, AGNOLOTTI, CAPPELLETTI ETC

HOW MUCH WE CAN SEE, BUT HOW MUCH MORE WE'RE BOUND TO MISS – ALAS! SO COME AGAIN!

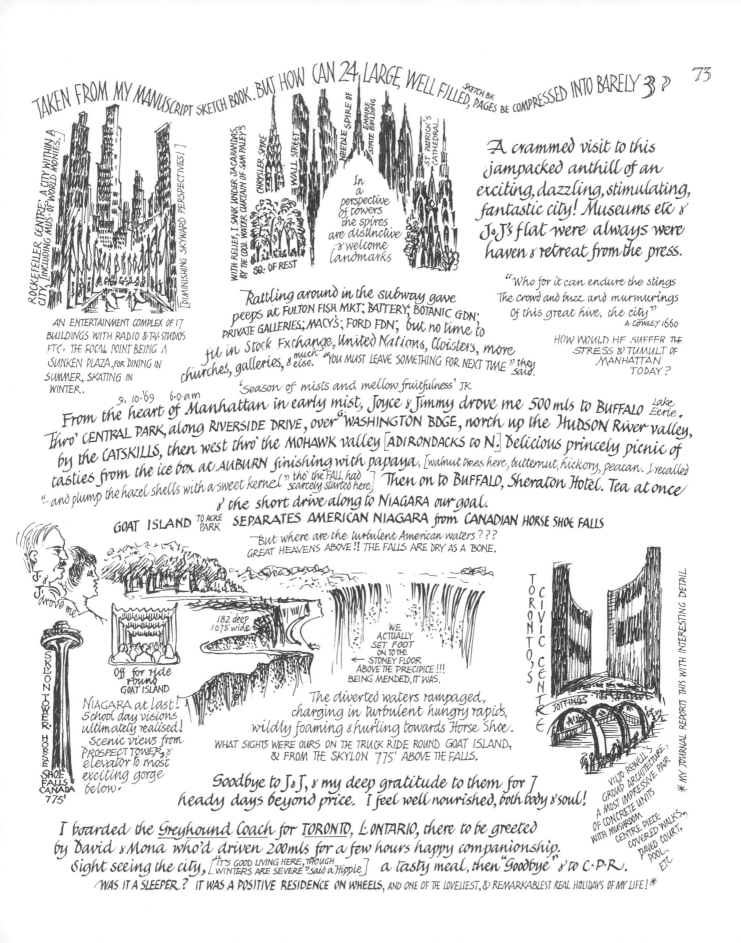

TAKEN FROM MY MANUSCRIPT SKETCH BOOK. BUT HOW CAN 24, LARGE, WELL FILLED, SKETCH BK PAGES BE COMPRESSED INTO BARELY 3?

ROCKEFELLER CENTRE: A CITY WITHIN A CITY, [INCLUDING MUS: OF WORLD MONIES.]

[DIMINISHING SKYWARD PERSPECTIVES]

CHRYSLER SPIRE

WALL STREET

NEEDLE SPIRE OF EMPIRE STATE BUILDING

ST PATRICK'S CATHEDRAL

WITH RELIEF, I SANK UNDER JACARANDAS, BY THE COOL WATER CURTAIN OF SAM PALEY'S SQ: OF REST

In a perspective of towers the spires are distinctive & welcome landmarks

AN ENTERTAINMENT COMPLEX OF 17 BUILDINGS WITH RADIO & T.V. STUDIOS ETC. THE FOCAL POINT BEING A SUNKEN PLAZA, FOR DINING IN SUMMER, SKATING IN WINTER.

A crammed visit to this jampacked anthill of an exciting, dazzling, stimulating, fantastic city! Museums etc & J&J's flat were always were haven & retreat from the press.

"Who for it can endure the stings
The crowd and buzz and murmurings
Of this great hive, the city"
A. COWLEY 1660

HOW WOULD HE SUFFER THE STRESS & TUMULT OF MANHATTAN TODAY?

Rattling around in the subway gave peeps at FULTON FISH MKT; BATTERY; BOTANIC GDN; PRIVATE GALLERIES; MACY'S; FORD FDN; but no time to fit in Stock Exchange, United Nations, Cloisters, more churches, galleries, & much else. "YOU MUST LEAVE SOMETHING FOR NEXT TIME" they said.

'Season of mists and mellow fruitfulness' JK

9. 10. '69   6.0. am

From the heart of Manhattan in early mist, Joyce & Jimmy drove me 500 mls to BUFFALO Lake Eerie. Thro' CENTRAL PARK, along RIVERSIDE DRIVE, over WASHINGTON BDGE, north up the HUDSON River valley, by the CATSKILLS, then west thro' the MOHAWK valley [ADIRONDACKS to N.] Delicious princely picnic of tasties from the ice box at AUBURN finishing with papaya, [walnut trees here, butternut, hickory, peacan. I recalled "- and plump the hazel shells with a sweet kernel" tho' the FALL had scarcely started here.] Then on to BUFFALO, Sheraton Hotel. Tea at once & the short drive along to NIAGARA our goal.

GOAT ISLAND TO ACRE PARK SEPARATES AMERICAN NIAGARA from CANADIAN HORSE SHOE FALLS

But where are the turbulent American waters ??? GREAT HEAVENS ABOVE !! THE FALLS ARE DRY AS A BONE.

J&J drove me

SKYLON TOWER. HORSE SHOE FALLS CANADA 775'

Off for ride round GOAT ISLAND

182' deep 1075' wide

NIAGARA at last! School day visions ultimately realised! Scenic views from PROSPECT TOWER, & elevator to most exciting gorge below.

WE ACTUALLY SET FOOT ON TO THE STONEY FLOOR ABOVE THE PRECIPICE !!! BEING MENDED, IT WAS.

The diverted waters rampaged, charging in turbulent hungry rapids, wildly foaming & hurling towards Horse Shoe. WHAT SIGHTS WERE OURS ON THE TRUCK RIDE ROUND GOAT ISLAND, & FROM THE SKYLON 775' ABOVE THE FALLS.

TORONTO'S CIVIC CENTRE

JOTTINGS

* MY JOURNAL REPORTS THIS WITH INTERESTING DETAIL

VILJO REVELL'S GROUP ARCHITECTURE, A MOST IMPRESSIVE PAIR OF CONCRETE UNITS WITH MUSHROOM CENTRE PIECE COVERED WALKS, PAVED COURT, POOL, ETC

Goodbye to J&J, & my deep gratitude to them for 7 heady days beyond price. I feel well nourished, both body & soul!

I boarded the Greyhound Coach for TORONTO, L ONTARIO, there to be greeted by David & Mona who'd driven 200mls for a few hours happy companionship. Sight seeing the city, [IT'S GOOD LIVING HERE, THOUGH WINTERS ARE SEVERE" said a Hippie] a tasty meal, then "Goodbye" & to C.P.R.
WAS IT A SLEEPER? IT WAS A POSITIVE RESIDENCE ON WHEELS, AND ONE OF THE LOVELIEST, & REMARKABLEST REAL HOLIDAYS OF MY LIFE! *

C·P·R· TO L· SUPERIOR & PRAIRIES

CANADIAN PACIFIC RAILWAY

MORE CHILDHOOD LONGINGS REALISED AT LAST!

12.10.69 Dear M & F, A paean of praise for this *Roomette* of the *C·P·R·*, a masterpiece of 'multum in parvo' planning, [bed, toilet, sitting room in one; bathroom down passage,] a window on the world, a little peacehaven, a time for cud-chewing & contemplation. Observation domes, coffee rooms, dining car, gave walking exercise as well as happy contacts with folk in relaxed mood. Frequently fed; 5 star menus best attention while the miles roll by. AN EXPERIENCE IN A CLASS OF ITS OWN · THANK YOU FOR RECOMMENDING IT, MURIEL.

After the TORONTO COACH via fruit areas, vineyards, orchards, pumpkin fields; this train snakes its way thro' conifer forests—& what engineering!!

NEAR BUFFALO — L·EERIE Humps to end all hump bridges, but sk: bk: not ready.

HAMILTON FLYOVER & L·ONTARIO & many yachts. We were up & over in a trice, & Hamilton passed

ONTARIO PROVINCE

"What a terrain of cliffs, ravines, rocks, rivers, falls! "LAND OF 1,000 LAKES."

I retired to a curtain of gold-tipped moonlit birches, & woke to a white world of snowy "Christmas" trees, the train threading its way among forests, lumber, lake waters, torrents, rocks. <u>LAKE HURON</u> now past, & here is <u>LAKE SUPERIOR</u>, & <u>THUNDER BAY</u> where I join M, & break for a spell with J & W. <u>A THANKSGIVING DAY</u> welcome, & dinner of celebration. "Our Xmas Dinner in advance" I thought:-

CANAPES; TURKEY, STUFFINGS, WINES, CRANBERRY, NUT, SAUCES, SWEET POTATO, SQUASH; BLUEBERRY PIE; PUMPKIN PIE, CREAM ETC

SKI BOOTS, SKATING BOOTS, CLIMBING BOOTS, SKIS, FOR THIS FAMILY OF 5, hung suspended from the cellar ceiling in J & W's home.

MT· McKAY 1010' & THE ROCKY HORIZON OF HILLS BEYOND FORT WILLIAM. [BALSAM POPLARS, SUGAR MAPLES, FIRE BIRCHES, TOBOGGAN RUNS]

KAKABEKA FALLS, reduced now to mere trickles by drought; no rushing torrents. So we searched for lichens, climbing among the dry boulders & clambering over rocks & stones.

J & W both of Lakehead University showed us round it. We toured by Indian Reserves, a beaver dam, Kakabeka Falls [clambered among rocks, drought dry] Mt McKay [the sugar maples yellow gold, each one a candle flame,] & Centennial Park, with log built bunk house, cook hse, wash-room etc, & lumber imaginatively set for fun & games.

STEPS UP TO THE LOG HOUSE — CENTENNIAL PARK — LOGS GALORE TO PLAY ON

TALL GRAIN ELEVATORS BREAK THE LEVEL LINES OF THE PRAIRIES.

Good companionship on board.

Oct 15. Goodbye to J & W, then, like greeting an old friend we climbed into the C·P·R· to cross the <u>PRAIRIES</u>. We slept, we ate, we read, we talked, surveying the moving scene in an orgy of blissful satisfaction. RETARD WATCHES. Hour after hour, mile after mile across the high grain plateau. 2,000' WERE WE BORED? No! My sketch pages are full. We woke to glowing sunrise, immense distances, biscuit-fawn under a blue cyclorama [what luck was ours,] the low slanting sun-rays catching each hump of contour across to the wide horizon. Occasional geese, duck, cattle, fire-watch towers, pulp mills, mining, lumber, pin pointed the miles. RETARD WATCHES.

I thought you'd like a few words. How v. disappointing I was not able to fit in a visit to you both in Arrowhead, Okemos.

With all good wishes Doris Ann G. P.T.O

MEDECIN HAT CATHEDRAL. Famous gas city. [Names fascinate: Kamininquia, Osagiqua, Red Jacket, Moose Jaw, Piapot, Swift Current.

SKEINS OF GEESE — NOW APPROACHING RANCH COUNTRY — ILLE CILLE WAET RIVER.

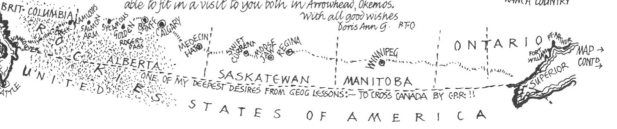

49° VANC ISLAND — BRIT· COLUMBIA — ROCKIES — ALBERTA — SASKATEWAN — MANITOBA — ONTARIO — MAP CONT'D SEATTLE — UNITED STATES — ONE OF MY DEEPEST DESIRES FROM GEOG LESSONS:— TO CROSS CANADA BY C·P·R· !!

KAMLOOPS, SALMON ARM, SICAMOUS, ROGERS PASS, GOLDEN, BANFF, CALGARY, MEDECIN HAT, SWIFT CURRENT, MOOSE JAW, REGINA, WINNIPEG, FORT WILLIAM, PT. ARTHUR, SUPERIOR

STATES OF AMERICA

LOFTY PEAKS & SHINING SNOW FIELDS ABOVE BLUE WATERS OF LAKE LOUISE.

INDIAN ENCAMPMENT OF TEEPEES, SEEN AS WE FLASHED BY [TRAIN]

Kindly & generous A.C. [sleeveless, the house so warm,] lived not in Wolf St., or Beaver St., Buffalo, Grizzly Lynx, or Marten St., but in Muskrat St. THE CHINOOK WIND IN WINTER, CAN RAISE TEMP FROM SUB ZERO TO THAW IN MINUTES!

SKY PRICKING, KINGLY CRAGS OF YOHO PARK.

CASCADE MT / AYLMER 10,375

THE BOW RIVER DRAWS BOWS ALONG ITS MOUNTAIN COURSE, RINGING BANFF EN ROUTE — BANFF

THE HOODOOS, STRANDED ROCK FIGURES CEMENTED PILLARS LEFT STANDING ON THE TERRACED HILLSIDE SCULPTURED BY THE GLACIAL DRIFT.

"DO NOT FEED THE BEARS"

YES, WE SAW BROWN BEARS AT OCCASIONAL PICNIC SPOTS

ELK SEEN FROM TRAIN

MAGNIFICENT BISON BANFF

P.S. "Look ahead! Look again! Is it a mirage?" Away breaking the level horizon, a line of snowy peaks! The ROCKIES to be sure — & here is CALGARY. Now for a winding course among the foothills & mighty peaks of BANFF.
Excitedly, D.

BANFF. Dear Janet & Brian,   16.10.69
What a vast map yours is!
At midnight [C·P·R] in WINNIPEG, & later in REGINA, I woke wishing I could leap across to see dimpled you, your family, & yr ploys in Saskatoon; so near yet so far — most tantalising.

Now here in sparkling BANFF, Ann Chapman is giving us luxury cherishing, as we roam this wonderful rock world of snowy peaks blue lakes, hot springs & romping torrents.

VANCOUVER
We left the C·P·R· at Banff, [it traverses much of the Rockies by night,] favouring day travel by coach thro' that tremendous scenery of mountain profiles, glaciers, chasms, rock palaces, embroideries in stone, frost filigrees, icicle curtains, diamond slopes, corridors of light; my travel journal is rapturous; a Kubla Khan of wonderment.
"------- ribbed and paled in With rocks unscalable and roaring waters" W·Sh

A night in CACHE CREEK Motel, then the day coach, eyes agog for the cascading races of the Thompson River as it piles into Hell's Gate & Devil's Wash Basin. Maple trees were temples of light on hillsides, rivers of gold in gullies; Fraser Gorge yellow, pink, copper, bronze, Indian red, this Fall. Towering Hiawatha country! An astonishing, ecstatic ride.
Thank you for suggesting the COACH journey to be a "MUST." The very best of good wishes, from, D·G.
SIDNEY B. ALSO SUGGESTED THE COACH.

Yet another view of the great molar peak of Eisenhower's Mt originally called THE CASTLE.

A bubble cable car gondola took us up to walk the crest of Sulphur Mt, then a dip in the Hot Sulphur Spring below. Air temp 32°. Water 102°!

LITTLE CHIPMUNKS, with black stripe backs, nervous & swift as a flash, sported high up on Sulphur Mtn.

MOUNTAINS OF THE GREAT DIVIDE; SNOWFIELDS, OBELISKS, CHIMNEYS & VICTORIA GLACIER. MY JOURNAL IS FULL OF MOUNTAIN SCAPES AND EULOGIES

saw tooth profiles / sun behind peak for a spell / icicle curtains
Spectacle after spectacle in this wide THEATRE OF THE ROCKIES.

[LICENSED MECHANIC & ENGINE ANALYSER APPROPRIATELY LOCATED HERE]

KEENLY ALERT / FELLOW TRAVELLERS THRO' THE ROCKIES / MUFFLED & SWATHED IN HIS PONCHO!

ROGERS' PASS MEMORIAL 5,000mls of TRANS CANADA HIGHWAY

SPECTACLES? FESTIVALS? ALAS NO
NO FOLK LORE, INDIAN FESTIVALS, RODEOS, STAMPEDES, MOUNTIES, AT THIS TIME OF YEAR. NOVEMBER

FORT WILLIAM / PORT ARTHUR / LAKE SUPERIOR / C A N A D A / MONTREAL / QUEBEC / RIVER ST LAWRENCE / NOVA SCOTIA / L. HURON / TORONTO / ONTARIO / LONDON / DETROIT / BUFFALO / L. MICHIGAN / CHICAGO / LAKE ERIE / U N I T E D   S T A T E S / BOSTON / NEW YORK / ATLANTIC OCEAN / COYOTE

YES, LAKES ON THE MAP, BUT GREAT SEAS IN REALITY

VANCOUVER
A FEW IMPRESSIONS

Sidney B, Betty F, & Nina greeted us. Torrents of rain, no half measures! But what hospitality! Sight-seeing drives; theatre & concert bookings; family gatherings; parties with friends; haute cuisine meals, also humble picnics; heights & panoramic views, all fitted in.

GILFORD ST VISTA. BOATS GALORE HERE IN VANCOUVER

GROUSE MT CHAIR-LIFT & SKYRIDE FOR GRAND VIEWS.

BETTY'S RELATIVES GATHERED TOGETHER A PARTY OF 25 FOLK TO MEET US & DINE IN THEIR MOST SUMPTUOUS CLIFF SIDE HOUSE, TERRACED & SEA GIRT, WITH TOTEMS AMONG THE TREES.

WHAT FALL COLOURS! DOGWOODS BLAZING RED ASPENS AMBER MAPLES YELLOW

DOMICAL GREEN HSE, ELIZABETH PARK. A must, this high view pt, for city, for the waters, the N. Shore mountains, with the lush Quarry Gdns below.

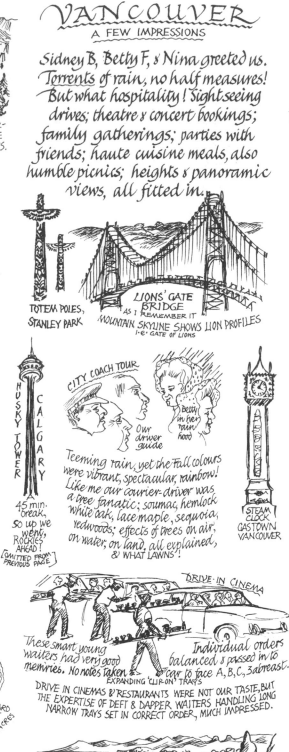

TOTEM POLES, STANLEY PARK

LIONS' GATE BRIDGE AS I REMEMBER IT MOUNTAIN SKYLINE SHOWS LION PROFILES i.e. GATE OF LIONS

QUEEN ELIZABETH THEATRE, THE SEAT OF VANCOUVER FESTIVAL & RENOWNED FOR ITS CONCERTS & PRODUCTIONS

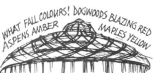

IN VANCOUVER, & ON THE C.P.R.

HOT, BROWN, CRUNCHY, RAISIN BUNS FOR BKFAST, & ON THE C.P.R.

A SOVEREIGN SALAD, 2nd TO NONE WOULD TEMPT FUSSIEST GOURMET. THEY HAVE EXPERTISE HERE! DOLLOPS OF GOOD COTT. CHEESE, & FRUITS OF EVERY VARIETY

VANCOUVER

STREET LAMP [MEMORY]

FIRE HYDRANT THESE IN PLENTY

HUSKY TOWER CALGARY A 45 min. break, so up we went. ROCKIES AHEAD! [OMITTED FROM PREVIOUS PAGE]

CITY COACH TOUR

Our driver guide

Betty in her rain hood

Teeming rain, yet the Fall colours were vibrant, spectacular, rainbow! Like me our courier-driver was a tree fanatic; soumac, hemlock, white oak, lace maple, sequoia, redwoods; effects of trees on air, on water, on land, all explained, & WHAT LAWNS!

STEAM CLOCK GASTOWN VANCOUVER

CANADIAN ESKIMO CARVINGS, their bulky rounded forms & smooth soapstone surfaces fascinated me.

PACIFIC OCEAN

BEACH STANLEY PARK PENINSULA

FIRST NARROWS

LIONS GATE

STANLEY PARK

BEAVER LAKE ZOO

BROCKTON POINT

LOST LAGOON

W. END

BURRARD INLET

1,000 ACRES

What foresight Mr Stanley! This wooded peninsula preserved as a natural amenity for all time! Only a stone's throw away, we dropped down by the LOST LAGOON, [alive with ducks, migrating geese.] →

DRIVE-IN CINEMA

These smart young waiters had very good memries. No notes taken.

Individual orders balanced & passed in to car to face A, B, C, 3 abreast.

EXPANDING 'CLIP-ON' TRAYS

DRIVE IN CINEMAS & RESTAURANTS WERE NOT OUR TASTE, BUT THE EXPERTISE OF DEFT & DAPPER WAITERS HANDLING LONG NARROW TRAYS SET IN CORRECT ORDER, MUCH IMPRESSED.

8 hired bikes to girdle the Park, exploring the bathing beaches, the unfenced Zoo, the boating lake, Totems, & the Pacific shore by Siwash Rock. POOLS GREAT TREE TRUNKS WASHED UP ON PACFIC SHORE

SEE JOURNAL FOR MANY MORE DETAILS

The effect looking across CAPILANO SUSPENSION BRIDGE. Dare we trust ourselves to this bouncing & swaying cakewalk? we did.

TO VANCOUVER ISLAND; VICTORIA; SEATTLE; YOSEMITE; G·CANYON; HAWAIAN ISLES HONOLULU; & FIJI ISLES.

HORSE SHOE BAY
N. VANCOUVER

7·0 a.m. Taxi to coach for Horse Shoe Bay, cherries flaming. Coach drives on to ferry. Bkfst on board. Vanc Isle ahead. Bus, jetty to Nanaimo; coach to Victoria.

LOGS, LOGS, & MORE LOGS. YOU CAN BARELY SEE WATER!

Memorable table-mats on board. V.G. Clam Chowder soup. Acres of deck, but few folk travelling this season.

PICTURE HERE — LEGENDE ABOVE

THE ISLANDS OF ACTIVE PASSAGE 2½ hrs of sheer pleasure, this homely return sail to Vancouver. 10 LIFE BOATS. UMPTEEN TOILETS.

In Vancouver, S·B. recommended the ferry for Vancouver Island, from Horse Shoe Bay to Nanaimo, & thence to Victoria. From there we flew to Verna & Jim in Seattle. Later, returning from Vanc·Island, the ferry Schwartz Bay to Twassassan, swishing between the islands of Active Passage currents gave us once again flavours of our W. Highland & Island sailings back home.

DOGWOOD FLOWERING TREE EMBLEM OF B.C.

FRIENDLY FOLK IN VANCOUVER Is. WELL WISHING FROM TAXI MAN, CUSTOMS OFFICER-WOMAN, FERRY OFFICIAL & SHIP'S WAITER

VICTORIA
Empress Hotel lunch. Harbour ships. Superb setting for B·C's capital city, ON THIS SOUTH PENINSULA OF THE ISLAND

VICTORIA ART GALLERY, impressive modern, with water garden of stones. Don't miss the superb Butchart Gdns, well worth taxi/coach drive

This is V&J's house SEATTLE above PUGET SOUND. V's food was epicurean & Fall colours truly remarkable [Japanese garden] Lake Washington's pontoon bridges; boats & boats; cars & cars; monorail above streets; a lattice of ugly overhead cables; the Space Needle; temperature clocks, etc…

Once over the American border, we craved a look at Yosemite National Park, & [dare we hope] the Grand Canyon of Colorado R. "But too late now. Season over. Date them for next yr & save up" we agreed.

Oh, those meadows & magnificent Sequoias of Yosemite! those sheer rock walls, peaks, domes, cascades, cataracts, rock sculptures, panoramic views above & below to the deep valley floors! of this great Sierra Nevada Range! Can there be more transcendent grandeur? A knockout tour beyond précis description; El Capitan's granite buttress 3604' from valley floor. We thought of our John Muir's classic writings on Sierra Nevada in 1911, also of our modest Quirang miniatures.

No room here for the GRAND CANYON of ARIZONA, that silver thread, walled in by ramparts in its deep abyss. FOR ME, BORN & REARED IN LONDON, THESE GEOLOGICAL SPECTACLES, REMARKABLE, UNFORGETABLE, WERE A STUNNING SIGHT "Then felt I like some watcher of the skies, When a new planet swims into his ken" J·Keats

QUANTAS PHONES? "CLOCKS RETARDED PLANE 1 HOUR" IS IT?) EARLY SO DON'T MISS IT STEAMING FACE CLOTHS PRESENTED

And now for the Hawaiian Islands, 6 of them, volcanic, with cliffs, craters, canyons, volcanoes, lava contortions, forest jungles; Hawaii's 8,000' Mt, Maui's Gt Crater; Oahu's Honolulu & Waikiki beach; Waimea's Canyon; Kauai [Captain Cook] & Lanai, the smallest. We like to think we spotted them all, & thought of Pearl Harbour, of Gauguin, & his evocative paintings.

NOW ACROSS THE EQUATOR INTO THE SOUTHERN HEMISPHERE, FOR FIJI ISLANDS — SOFT VOICES OF SWARTHY FIJIANS, WHITE ROBED, THEIR KINDLY ATTENTIONS — HIBISCUS FLAMING, BOUGAINVILLEA CASCADING; FRANGIPANI FRAGRANT; TURQUOISE SEAS; SAND BEACHES; & SO TO NEW ZEALAND.

ONE PONDERS:- "WHAT IS MAN THAT THOU ART MINDFUL OF HIM?"

NEW ZEALAND
JUST A PEEP.

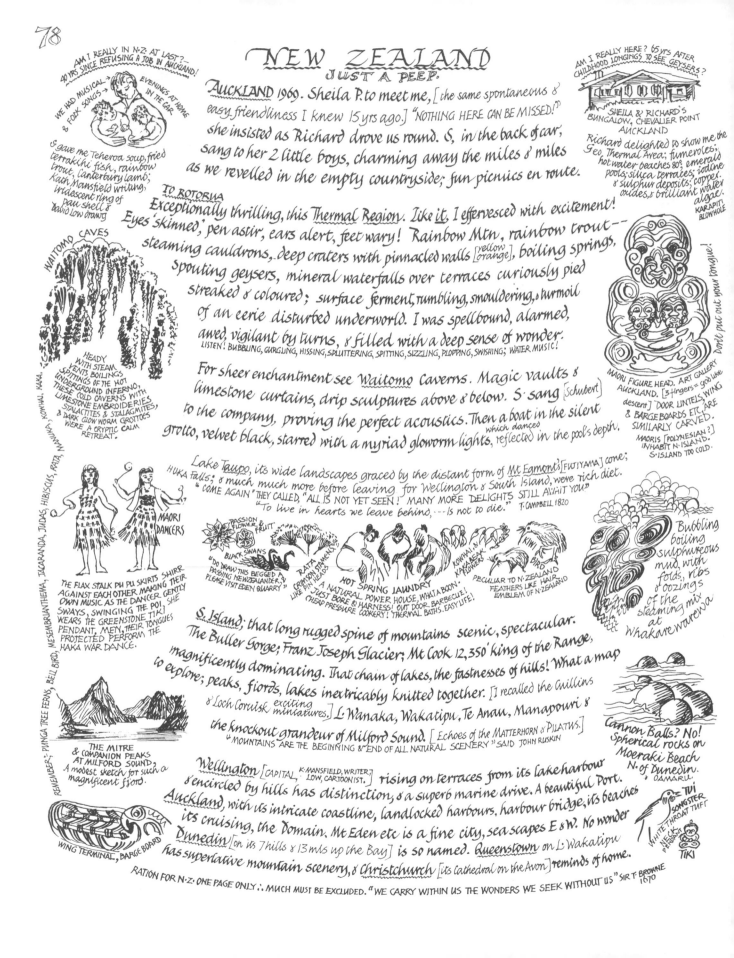

AM I REALLY IN N.Z. AT LAST?— 40 YRS SINCE REFUSING A JOB IN AUCKLAND!

WE HAD MUSICAL FOLK SONGS → EVENINGS AT HOME IN THE CAR.

S. gave me Teheroa soup, fried terrakihi fish, rainbow trout, Canterbury lamb; Kath, Mansfield writing; iridescent ring of paua shell & David Low drawing

AM I REALLY HERE? 65 YRS AFTER CHILDHOOD LONGINGS TO SEE GEYSERS?

SHEILA & RICHARD'S BUNGALOW, CHEVALIER POINT AUCKLAND

Richard delighted to show me the Geo. Thermal Area; fumeroles; hot water beaches 80°; emerald pools; silica terraces; iodine & sulphur deposits; copper oxides, & brilliant water algae. KARAPITI BLOWHOLE

AUCKLAND 1969. Sheila P. to meet me, [the same spontaneous & easy friendliness I knew 15 yrs ago.] "NOTHING HERE CAN BE MISSED!" she insisted as Richard drove us round. S. in the back of car, sang to her 2 little boys, charming away the miles & miles as we revelled in the empty countryside; fun picnics en route.

TO ROTORUA
Exceptionally thrilling, this Thermal Region. Like it, I effervesced with excitement! Eyes 'skinned', pen astir, ears alert, feet wary! Rainbow Mtn, rainbow trout— steaming cauldrons, deep craters with pinnacled walls [yellow orange], boiling springs, spouting geysers, mineral waterfalls over terraces curiously pied streaked & coloured; surface ferment, rumbling, smouldering, & turmoil of an eerie disturbed underworld. I was spellbound, alarmed, awed, vigilant by turns, & filled with a deep sense of wonder.
LISTEN! BUBBLING, GURGLING, HISSING, SPLUTTERING, SPITTING, SIZZLING, PLOPPING, SWISHING; WATER MUSIC!

WAITOMO CAVES

HEADY WITH STEAM VENTS, BOILINGS SPITTINGS OF THE HOT UNDERGROUND INFERNO, THESE COLD CAVERNS WITH LIMESTONE EMBROIDERIES, STALACTITES & STALAGMITES, & DARK GLOW WORM GROTTOES WERE A CRYPTIC CALM RETREAT.

For sheer enchantment see Waitomo Caverns. Magic vaults & limestone curtains, drip sculptures above & below. S. sang [Schubert] to the company, proving the perfect acoustics. Then a boat in the silent grotto, velvet black, starred with a myriad glowworm lights, which dances reflected in the pool's depth.

MAORI FIGURE HEAD. ART GALLERY AUCKLAND. [3 fingers = god like descent] DOOR LINTELS, WING & BARGEBOARDS ETC. ARE SIMILARLY CARVED.
MAORIS [POLYNESIAN?] INHABIT N. ISLAND. S. ISLAND TOO COLD. Don't put out your tongue!

MAORI DANCERS

THE FLAX STALK PU PU SKIRTS SHIRR AGAINST EACH OTHER MAKING THEIR OWN MUSIC AS THE DANCER GENTLY SWAYS, SWINGING THE POI. SHE WEARS THE GREENSTONE TIKI PENDANT. MEN, THEIR TONGUES PROJECTED PERFORM THE HAKA WAR DANCE.

REMEMBER:- PUNGA TREE FERNS, BELL BIRD, MESEMBRIANTHEMA, JACARANDA, JUDAS, HIBISCUS, RATA, MANUKA, KOWHAI, KAKA.

Lake Taupo, its wide landscapes graced by the distant form of Mt Egmont's [FUJIYAMA] cone; HUKA FALLS; & much much more before leaving for Wellington & South Island, were rich diet. "COME AGAIN" THEY CALLED, "ALL IS NOT YET SEEN! MANY MORE DELIGHTS STILL AWAIT YOU" "To live in hearts we leave behind,---Is not to die." T. CAMPBELL 1820

PASSION FLOWER & FRUIT
BLACK SWANS
"DO DRAW THIS BEGGED A PASSING NEW ZEALANDER" PLEASE VISIT EDEN QUARRY.
RATA CRIMSON TUMENT & LIKE PIN HEADS
HOT SPRING LAUNDRY
A NATURAL POWER HOUSE, WHAT A BOON. JUST BORE & HARNESS! OUT DOOR BARBECUE! CHEAP PRESSURE COOKERY! THERMAL BATHS. EASY LIFE!
KOWHAI, N. KAKA BEAK FLOWERS
KIWI BIRD
PECULIAR TO N. ZEALAND FEATHERS LIKE HAIR. EMBLEM OF N. ZEALAND.

Bubbling boiling sulphureous mud, with folds, ribs & oozings of the steaming mix at Whakarewarewa

S. Island; that long rugged spine of mountains scenic, spectacular. The Buller Gorge; Franz Joseph Glacier; Mt Cook 12,350' king of the Range, magnificently dominating. That chain of lakes, the fastnesses of hills! What a map to explore; peaks, fiords, lakes inextricably knitted together. [I recalled the Cuillins & Loch Coruisk exciting miniatures.] L. Wanaka, Wakatipu, Te Anau, Manapouri & the knockout grandeur of Milford Sound. [Echoes of the MATTERHORN & PILATUS.] "MOUNTAINS ARE THE BEGINNING & END OF ALL NATURAL SCENERY" SAID JOHN RUSKIN

THE MITRE & COMPANION PEAKS AT MILFORD SOUND. A modest sketch for such a magnificent fiord.

Cannon Balls? No! Spherical rocks on Moeraki Beach N. of Dunedin. & OAMARU

Wellington [CAPITAL, K. MANSFIELD, WRITER; LOW, CARTOONIST.] rising on terraces from its lake harbour & encircled by hills has distinction, & a superb marine drive. A beautiful Port. Auckland, with its intricate coastline, landlocked harbours, harbour bridge, its beaches its cruising, the Domain. Mt Eden etc is a fine city, sea scapes E & W. No wonder Dunedin [on its 7 hills & 13 mls up the Bay] is so named. Queenstown on L. Wakatipu has superlative mountain scenery, & Christchurch [its Cathedral on the Avon] reminds of home.

WING TERMINAL, BARGE BOARD

TUI SONGSTER WHITE THROAT TUFT NEW UK PENDANT. TIKI

RATION FOR N.Z. ONE PAGE ONLY ∴ MUCH MUST BE EXCLUDED. "WE CARRY WITHIN US THE WONDERS WE SEEK WITHOUT US" SIR T. BROWNE 1670

FROM ONE SUPERB HARBOUR TO THE NEXT

GOODBYE TO AUCKLAND VISTAS; TASMAN SEA TO W- PACIFIC TO E; MT VICTORIA, THE BARRIERS, WHANGAROA, RANGITOTO, CORAMANDEL.

NOW FOR THE FLIGHT TO SYDNEY, AUSTRALIA.

THE GREAT SINGLE SPAN ARCH OF THE HARBOUR BRIDGE ABOVE SPARKLING WATERS OF THIS BUSY PORT

SYDNEY

BAYS & PENINSULAS OF N- BANK TO MANLY PT.

BAYS & PENINSULAS OF S- BANK TO THE HEADS.

8.0 PM
DIANA'S ICED SOUP SERVED ON THE TERRACE, DARLING PT, ABOVE TWINKLING HARBOUR LIGHTS, IS A VERY SPECIAL & TREASURED MEMORY

LUSCIOUS CANTALOUP MELONS REGALED US BETWEEN DIPS AT COLLAROY BEACH N OF SYDNEY,

& SWIFT LITTLE HONEY SUCKERS IN FLOWERY GARDENS, WERE JOLLY NOTES IN A VERY GOOD DAY

Diana W. to meet us [with bouquets; she, pretty as a picture, & just as bvts ago — now the apple of her husband's eye, - - - -] & keenly ready to escort & show us all the city's sights :-
THE STUPENDOUS HARBOUR;
[THE HEART, THE VERY CORE OF SYDNEY;]
the Harbour Bridge; [Old coat hanger] the Opera House; both symbols, as are :- Tower Bridge, Eiffel Tower; Parthenon; Taj Mahal.
Circular Quay, boating & cruises; Fort Denison [Pinch Gut;]
The Rocks water front & Argyle Arts Centre; the Bays & 34 superb beaches; [look out! shark infested waters!] 150ml shoreline. The Hydrofoil to the Heads & Manley Point was D's trump card & harbour climax.

Then :- A M.T Bdg view; later Centre Point Complex Tower, with Revolving Restaurant; R. Botanic Gardens; The Domain; Hyde Park; King's X; [Greenwich Village? Soho?] The Boomerang School; Rushcutter's & Elizabeth Bays, etc. From this pulsating city centre, & its external sprawl, we later retreated. Guess how—

SHELL HOODS & WINGS

SYDNEY'S OPERA HOUSE

Winged, hooded, cowled; is it a jostle of nuns; a billow of sails; a posse of shells; a muster of hoods; a parabolic cluster? THIS OPERA HOUSE CHANGES FROM EACH VIEWPOINT.

YACHTS IN RUSHCUTTERS BAY.
I wanted to visit all the bays of this hilly harbour coast, each having its own character.

By train! Yes, an OZ train north. 6 hrs, 210mls via TAREE to WINGHAM [Manning River] & the kind hospitality of our erstwhile neighbours Dr Ian & Hilda S, joining in their family life with beach barbecues, swimming, fishing, gold panning, fossicking & such zestful OZ pleasures. Did we see native reserves? Yes; vineyards? Yes; oyster beds? Yes; tropical storms? hailstones? Yes, a ballet of dancing ice balls in tumultuous bombardment. Where was the parched landscape we expected? This was a green countryside, pastoral, fertile; wattle & eucalypts scenting the air.

KOOKA BURRA'S

SIGNATURE TUNE :-
A LOW WARBLE, RISES LIKE BUBBLY BOILINGS, GOBBLINGS POPPING CORKS, THRO' CACKLING & SQUAWKING TO A MAGNIFICENT CRESCENDO & FALLING RALLENTANDO.
Mr Felix, our childhood raconteur, could imitate it. "They walk upside down in Australia" he said, "& sausages grow on trees."

FLYING FOXES - or FRUIT BATS, emerged from WINGHAM BRUSH' AT SUNSET IN HUNDREDS — BLACKENING THE SKY IN SILENT FLIGHT TO THEIR FEEDING GROUNDS. AN IMPRESSIVE SIGHT.

Idyllic green peninsula of CROWDY HEAD VILLAGE!

Here we relaxed; bathed in the long white rollers of 2 deserted beaches; drew in the little fishing harbour; climbed to the hilltop lighthouse.
2 SKETCHES WON 2 BOTTLES OF WINE.

Victorian Post Box

The Rocks Sydney

Barbecue picnics sausages, chops, & sizzling above the brazier

the fish we caught groper, schapper etc.

sun shades essential

Blackhead sand beach - miles of it, ½ hr from Wingham, gave bathing, leap frog, hopscotch, ballet, rocks for fishing, — all blissful till gathering black clouds bucketted hailstones!

Back in SYDNEY; (after the GT. B. REEF — [the fulfilment of a childhood desire longingly awaited,] — its coral cays, its blue lagoons, ebbtide pools, white breakers, island cliffs, shining beaches. blissful bathes, glass bottom boats & wonder water worlds — expensive tour but unforgettable;) we hired from AVIS ARK 123. [what did this number portend?] D. led us thro' the city centre & its outlying sprawl, then we set off for her cottage 'Agrapatna' in the Blue Mountains.

AN INFINITY OF SHAPES, THE MIND BOGGLES

A forest world of decorative corals, very sharp so wear waders

GT. BARRIER REEF

TEEMING FISH, EXQUISITE, SWIFT, SUDDEN & NEVER A COLLISION!

FISH WITH GOGGLE EYES, FISH WITH BEARDS & EVERY FASHION IN DRESS!

GT. BARRIER REEF

Alas! Climbing a long hill up thro' the dripping bush our ARK 123 petered out, & died. Why? oh why? No investigation, no coaxing availed. Our spirits sank to zero. Sunday morning pleasure cars streamed splashing by. Would none respond to our flagging down? Decoys?? A grim hour dragged. From the bush cicadas shrilled in chorus, frogs croaked BREK-A-KEK KEK IN DOUBLE BASE ; Eventually, mercifully, a car stopped, [humble family, returning with car load from furniture dump.]
B U T : THE DRIVER

ARK 123

Our little ARK 123 after initial bad luck, proved to be a treasure.

CICADAS, FROG

THE BUSH ORCHESTRA IN FULL PERSISTENT "SONG" THIS SUNDAY MORNING

recklessly made a U turn to flank us, — woe is me! accursed spite! a police car appeared & copped my Good Samaritan, fining him on the spot. No pleading, no 'HAVE MERCY,' no 'DAMSELS IN DISTRESS', could soften the hearts of those cops. Happily my £20 from a painting sale met his fine & he towed us along to KATOOMBA. What was wrong? Oh! AVIS! You gave us a broken petrol gauge which still registered 'Full'. We struggled no further but spent the night in Katoomba

THE FAMILY. Our Blessed Saviours. They furnished the family home by weekly visits to the local dump. Today's haul was picture frames.

Grace-ful trees. There are some 500 species of eucalypts (gums) native to Aust. The leathery grey leaves give off a mist of minute oil droplets, fragrant, & trunks ooz gum.

AHEAD WE SAW THE VAGUE MIST VEILED HORIZON OF THE BLUE MOUNTAINS

A ROUGH PLAN OF THE BLUE MTS PLATEAU

GORDON FALLS, DEEP FACE, GIANT STAIRWAY, KATOOMBA FALLS, SUBLIME PT, 3 SISTERS, HORSESHOE FALLS, SOLITARY, ECHO POINT, PULPIT HILL, PARRY'S LOOKDOWN, AMPHITHEATRE, LYELL'S CROSSING, THE PINNACLES, PADLEY'S PEDESTAL, KATOOMBA

HIGH AREAS 3,500 & CLIFFS, GORGES, RAVINES, LAWSON'S SUGAR LOAF, PERRY'S LOOKDOWN, GOVETT'S LEAP

THIS ROUGH MAP REMINDS US OF THE FALLS, ROCK FORMS, LOOKDOWNS, WHICH MIST HID AWAY FROM US, & DRAMATIC DROPS.

AUST. BLUE BELL

The Blue Mts Pioneer Rd keeps high, exciting engineering, steady run down to plain between woodland verges & drifts of golden coreopsis.

3 SISTERS we descried them thro' the mist, rising from the chasm

[But we were not done with police. "ROAD IN FLOOD," "BRIDGE WASHED AWAY", "DIVERSION"— Police stations consulted, [convicts visible behind bars.] Was there a route to Freeman's Reach? Our map foxed them. Dare we risk dirt roads? bush roads? Once there should we find lethal red back spiders in the loo, or lurking snakes in wait? "FAINT HEART NEVER WON FAIR LADY" we urged " DARE! THIS IS NED KELLY'S COUNTRY!"]

From D's cottage we explored the Blue Mts. Don't look for peaks. There are none. This is an upland plateau, bush covered, broken by a jigsaw of cliffs & canyons. Like Yosemite? No! Colorado? No! Views above dramatic drops? Yes. But eerie, mist shrouded views, today, rock phantoms, grey not blue. [Sunlight on oily eucalypt leaves gives the blue aura.]
HOW WILL THIS LANDSCAPE COMPARE WITH THE SNOWY MTS?

A PATCHWORK OF SNOW REMNANTS JUST BELOW THE 7000' SKYLINE. LIKE TORN WHITE RAGS, LAY ON THE SNOWY MTS RAMSHEAD RANGE & MT KOSCIUSKO. THESE ARE THE ONLY SNOW MTS IN AUSTRALIA.

We drove on to CANBERRA [2,000] the spacious stately purpose built Garden City Capital, down double & triple tree lined boulevards of impressive buildings; a city ringed by a blue horizon of hills, & came to the suburban homely welcome of Rosie & Robin [& toddler Michael] in Torrens.

Bungalows here have large front gardens; & the fanciful variety of letter boxes confounded me, giving many an appreciative giggle. The Gov.t presents 50 trees & bushes to each 1st time buyer.

We breezed along Lake Burley Griffin, [22 mls of shore line] with its Carillon Bell Tower, Capt.n Cook Memorial & Globe. We climbed Look Outs for views; visited Tidbinbilla Nature Reserve, & up by gum & fir forests to Bulls Head; Cotter Dam picnic; draw; Murumbidgee in full spate. My sketch book shows impassable fords, stormy landscapes.

Glass, Wood, brick, metal, concrete, plastic, petrol tin, fox. — Letters, news?, Milk, hosepipe all join in!

20 10 30 28 23 15

LETTER BOXES! A study in self expression! individuality in "DO IT YOURSELF." I idled away a Sunday morning, entertained by these revealing jobs!

EMU IN TIDBINBILLA Nature RESERVE.

FIRES & FOOLS ARE FOES OF THE FOREST

WATER CATCHMENT. KEEP AREA CLEAN

NO FLAME NO BLAME

PREVENT DESPAIR USE FIRE WITH CARE

A CARELESS MATCH & FIRE WILL CATCH

STOW IT DON'T THRO' IT

In this weather, fires had little chance! A dry parched OZ we did not see.

Toddler Michael — tries out my eight shoes

'Roos, fun to try & draw them. in the N. Reserve

☆   ☆   ☆   ☆

THE SNOWY MTS TOUR
HYDRO ELECTRIC SCHEME,

showed us the rolling skyline of the Great Divide, & long tattered snow remnants on Mt Kosciusko & alpine flowers. No peaks at all as Swiss Alps, Dolomites, Rockies, Parnassus or our Cuillin. Up thro' gum forests we went, then hair raising descents, into tunnels, saw great turbines, out by reservoirs & along by olives vineyards, orchards, to canneries in this green rural countryside. Then back to Canberra, & a warm THANK YOU to R & R for home from home, A.C.T.

YELLOW BUTTERFLIES ON THE SNOW. SILVER WHITE SNOW DAISIES. My sketch book is lyrical on the flowers, mountain gums snow gums. Very hot, oh the flies! & v. cold by night.

THE SKI LIFT, THREDBO, gave a refreshing walk. Later, above the snow line, on Mt Kosciusko 7514 we paddled in the swift clear shallow waters of the infant Snowy River

GOODBYE NOW TO N·S·W· & ON TO VICTORIA GARDEN STATE

MELBOURNE on the YARRA. Alan my nephew Dorothy & family to meet & welcome us. Paella, oysters, prawns, carpet bag steaks, pavlovas, passion fruit, excellent table. A free & easy well appointed home with pool. Eagerly they showed the handsome city centre (19. [Gold Rush Rags to Riches] I recalled] I enjoyed the Parks & Commemorative Avenue R·B·G· MELBA, TENNYSON, PADEREWSKI, ETC, the Sydney Myers Music Bowl Concert, Victorian Arts Centre, [stained glass roof,] Gog & Magog striking hours. R. Arcade; & bike track along the Yarra.

Dandenong Ranges, only 22m away with bush walks, lookouts, lakes, lyre birds, puffing Billyetc; Fairy Penguins of Philip Island; The Prom; beaches; all part of their background, & how well they've settled into it. Au revoir A & D. & & THANK YOU.

WILL RICKETT SANCTUARY Aboriginal faces carved in the rough stone face of the cliff. Dandenongs.

KOALA BEAR There he was in the gum trees, vegetarian, & original of the teddy bear.

LYRE BIRD 8 gallened quills 2 white quills 6, 7, 8, open quills a small bird.

WE'RE QUITE DISORIENTATED! THE MOON IS UPSIDE DOWN → JULY 20 1969 "ONE SMALL STEP FOR MAN BUT A GIANT LEAP FOR MANKIND"

CATTLE FARM NR. TO URYARRA.

THE SUN IS NOW IN THE NORTH; WE HAVE LOST THE PLOUGH & CANNOT FIND THE SOUTHERN CROSS!

ADELAIDE. S. AUST. Are we to go? The pressing invitation of June & Bill, [GEOGRAPHERS. We last met 6 yrs ago in Athens] & the vivid descriptions of these unquenchable enthusiasts, decided us.

"The sq. ml of the gracious city centre on our lovely Torrens R" they wrote, "is ringed by a green belt of parkland, & backed by the LOFTY RANGES, [2300. only 20 mins from city centre] just your meat. The exciting modern Festival Centre* famed far & wide, must be seen, [architects' pram hoods they seemed to me.] & we'll fatten you on J's splendid continental cooking; German wurst, Greek olives, Murray schnapper, French cheeses etc. You'll see the Flinders Rgs, enjoy our beaches, drive to Kangaroo Island & cruise the Murray River."

*HEXAGONAL WINDOWLESS CONCRETE & GLASS TENT SHAPED CANOPIES

"Then we'll take you to see that monolith, the largest "pebble" in the world, AYERS ROCK 1ml x 2mls. It rises abruptly from the scrub plain, a monster hog's back, scored, cavernous, & with wall paintings. Walking under its shadow is awe inspiring, haunting, Then at sunset it is a mighty spectacle, never to be forgotten; magnificent, bewitching in the splendour of its colour changes. Only 20 mls W are the OLGAS, 30 domed monoliths, one higher than Ayers, puddings of sandstone, Nature's sculpture, ravines between. You, being a sculptor, must see these."

"Then we'll wave you off to TASMANIA. In HOBART you'll see José & family who will proudly show off the splendid harbour 12mls up the Derwent Estuary & backed by the grandeur of Mt Wellington, 4165'. The 'Sailing City;' the 'SYDNEY-HOBART' Yacht Race; many fine beaches; Kelly's steps from Battery Pt. to Salamanca Place; Tasman Bridge; Parks; Claremont Choc Factory; its fine site; heaps to see; no slums poverty & they certainly know how to welcome & entertain visitors in Hobart & around the apple orchard isle, 200 x 200 mls "

"More of Nature's Sculpture for you in the geo formations at Eagle Hawk Neck on the way to PORT ARTHUR, There you will wince at the sad history of 'Man's inhumanity to Man.'"

"Please, come & see all for yourself. We'd so enjoy the pleasure of touring you as you did us. J & B"

How curious

these bush & cave ptgs

copied from

10 dollar notes.

"curiouser & curiouser"

I thought while copying

these primitive drawings

N.B. FOR YULE LOGS HERE THEY USE SLOW BURNING MALLEE ROOT- A SPECIES OF GUM

YES, A VAST CONTINENT, NEARLY 3,000,000 SQ MILES!! 2,500 MLS APP. ACROSS

OF AUSTRALIA'S VAST CONTINENT HOW LITTLE WE SAW, YET HOW MUCH IT WAS TO US.

20 —

NORTHERN TERRITORY

WESTERN AUSTRALIA

QUEENSLAND

SOUTH AUSTRALIA

BRISBANE

30 — INDIAN OCEAN

PERTH FREEMANTLE

NEW SOUTH WALES

WINGHAM

SYDNEY

GT. BARRIER
TOWNSVILLE
REEF
— 20

PACIFIC OCEAN

40 — — 500 mls to 1cm approx

ADELAIDE
MELB
VICTORIA

TASMAN SEA

NEW ZEALAND
AUCK LAND

HOBART

To see on this tour so many widely scattered friends in their settings abroad was most heart warming. [This one can never foretell.]

[What, of all these travels will the latent memory surprise us by suddenly revealing in later years?]

"Big things pass, little things remain," said R.K. "Wattle was all Australia to me."

[HOW MUCH WE WISHED IT WERE POSSIBLE TO DROP INTO ISPAHAN ON OUR RETURN JOURNEY!]

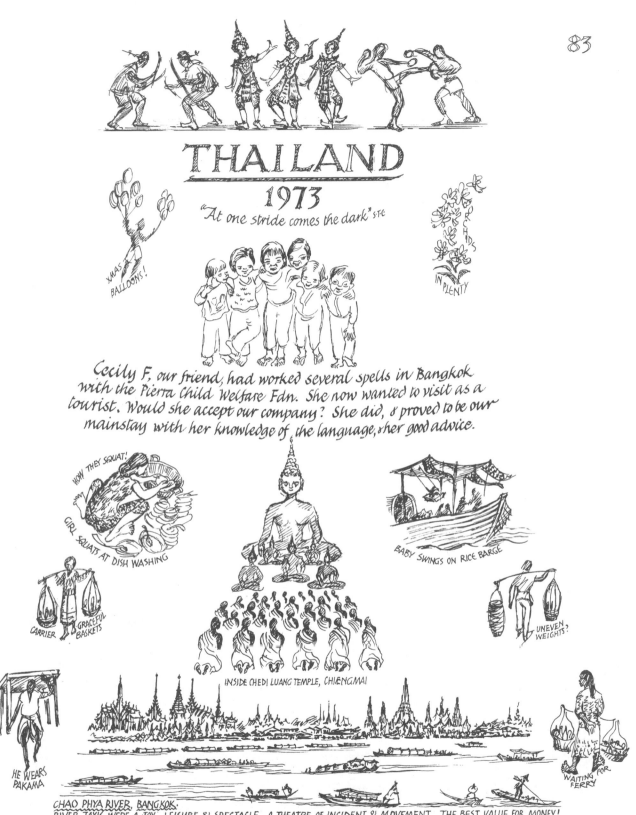

THAILAND
1973
"At one stride comes the dark" S.T.C.

XMAS BALLOONS!

ORCHIDS IN PLENTY

Cecily F., our friend, had worked several spells in Bangkok with the Pierra Child Welfare Fdn. She now wanted to visit as a tourist. Would she accept our company? She did, & proved to be our mainstay with her knowledge of the language, & her good advice.

HOW THEY SQUAT!
GIRL SQUATS AT DISH WASHING

BABY SWINGS ON RICE BARGE

CARRIER GRACEFUL BASKETS

UNEVEN WEIGHTS?

INSIDE CHEDI LUANG TEMPLE, CHIENGMAI

HE WEARS PAKAMA

WAITING FOR FERRY

CHAO PHYA RIVER, BANGKOK:
RIVER TAXIS WERE A JOY, LEISURE & SPECTACLE, A THEATRE OF INCIDENT & MOVEMENT, THE BEST VALUE FOR MONEY!
A FEW BAHT TOOK YOU CRISS CROSSING WITH LOCAL FOLK & BUDDHIST MONKS COMING ON, & GETTING OFF; VENDORS, PEDLARS,
CITY MEN, MUMS & BABIES. WAT ARUN TEMPLE TO W, PRANGS SPARKLING IN MAJESTY; WAT PRA KEOW TO E. A CLUSTER OF SPIRES & TRIPLE ROOFS. SUPER!
FOR A SPIRE ADDICT, COULD THERE BE ANYTHING BETTER? THE ROYAL TEMPLE OF EMERALD BUDDHA HAD A PROLIFERATION.

IN THE COMPOUND OF
WAT PHRA KEO
THE TEMPLE OF
THE EMERALD BUDDHA

Little bells fringe the eaves of compound buildings giving out various tinkling notes with every breeze. Their gilded tongues glitter & twinkle in the brilliant sunlight.

I had a pair of persistent black eyes peering over my shoulder as I drew. He left, then returned at regular intervals to witness progress, & to measure my drawing as it were against the realities. Then pronounced in his limited English:-
"IT IS GOOD VERY GOOD."

WALL OF ROYAL TEMPLE

MOUNT STEPS BETWEEN PALMS ON TO WIDE PORTICO. REMOVE FOOTWEAR, MOUNT MARBLE STEPS, & STEAL INSIDE.

A Marble staircase leads up to the PANTHEON with its twin double gables & mosaic inlays aglow [ONE OF THE CETIYA SPIRE RISES BEHIND]

I have peace of mind for these drawings now. Cecily will call for me after 20 busily scribbling minutes.

We're on our own. No sight seeing party to keep up with!
As an inveterate doodler & spire addict, these subjects were just my meat. I drew with feverish delight as I contemplated this outpouring of craftsmanship in such graceful forms, rich with coloured glass mosaic, porcelain tiles, sculptures & gilding.

One could never draw fast enough such compelling subjects. Why not click a camera? Drawing makes one scrutinise, forcing close attention to the living moment. Better a few lines than a blank page. The slightest scribble can provide a clue, evoke a memory, but a blank page stands for nothing except 'lost for ever' opportunities, & these were once in a lifetime breathless sights. I felt like saying to that pair of black eyes "HAVE A GO YOURSELF, MY GOOD MAN"

Two of the Mums on the river taxi

MANY SUCH SCENES KEPT THE PEN VERY BUSY.

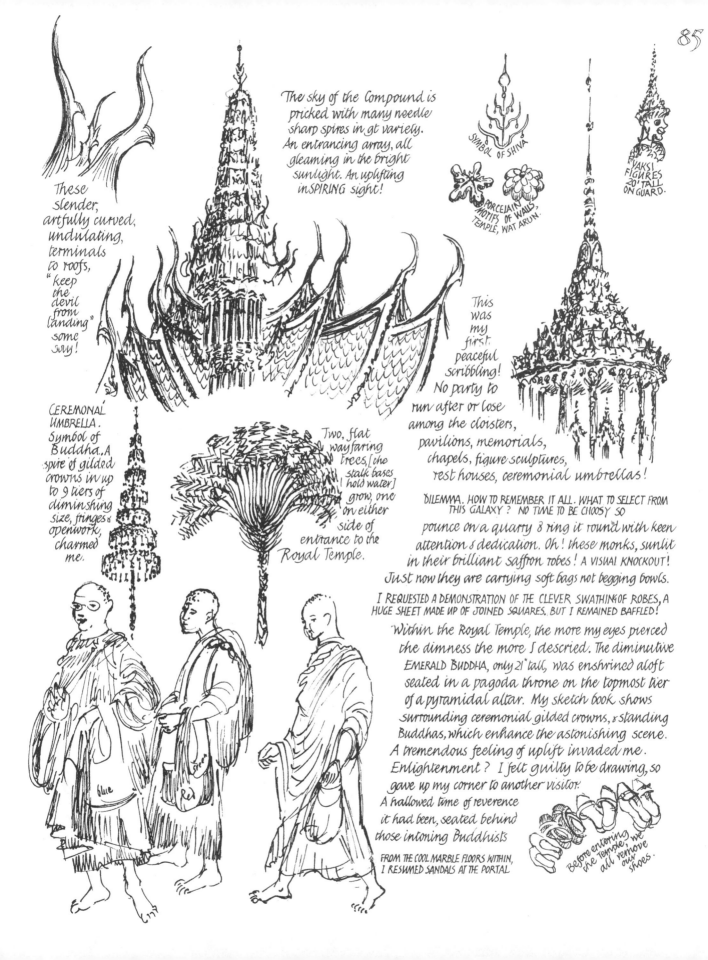

These slender, artfully curved, undulating, terminals to roofs, "keep the devil from landing" some say!

The sky of the Compound is pricked with many needle sharp spires in gt variety. An entrancing array, all gleaming in the bright sunlight. An uplifting inSPIRING sight!

SYMBOL OF SHIVA

PORCELAIN MOTIFS OF WALLS, TEMPLE, WAT ARUN.

YAKSI FIGURES 20' TALL ON GUARD.

This was my first peaceful scribbling! No party to run after or lose among the cloisters, pavilions, memorials, chapels, figure sculptures, rest houses, ceremonial umbrellas!

CEREMONIAL UMBRELLA. Symbol of Buddha. A spire of gilded crowns in up to 9 tiers of diminishing size, fringes & openwork, charmed me.

Two, flat wayfaring trees, [the stalk bases hold water] grow, one on either side of entrance to the Royal Temple.

DILEMMA. HOW TO REMEMBER IT ALL. WHAT TO SELECT FROM THIS GALAXY? NO TIME TO BE CHOOSY SO pounce on a quarry & ring it round with keen attention & dedication. Oh! these monks, sunlit in their brilliant saffron robes! A VISUAL KNOCKOUT! Just now they are carrying soft bags not begging bowls.

I REQUESTED A DEMONSTRATION OF THE CLEVER SWATHING OF ROBES, A HUGE SHEET MADE UP OF JOINED SQUARES. BUT I REMAINED BAFFLED!

Within the Royal Temple, the more my eyes pierced the dimness the more I descried. The diminutive EMERALD BUDDHA, only 21" tall, was enshrined aloft seated in a pagoda throne on the topmost tier of a pyramidal altar. My sketch book shows surrounding ceremonial gilded crowns, & standing Buddhas, which enhance the astonishing scene. A tremendous feeling of uplift invaded me. Enlightenment? I felt guilty to be drawing, so gave up my corner to another visitor.

A hallowed time of reverence it had been, seated behind those intoning Buddhists

FROM THE COOL MARBLE FLOORS WITHIN, I RESUMED SANDALS AT THE PORTAL

blue

Red

Before entering the Temple, we all remove our shoes.

FLOATING MARKET

What a sight! No photo could equal the reality of this living lively trading, the klong agog with sampans, sunshades, straw hats. A theme of circles & curves, a concourse of colour as I looked down from the bridge above.

A thrilling subject! Quick! catch it! Mind, don't catch it! Mind, don't back into the water! Tune in! Get the essence! She's going! Can't draw fast enough! She's gone!

Such fruits of the earth for sale! water melons, coconuts, cucumbers, papaya, peppers, pineapples, pomelos, bananas, mangoes, durian, beans, greens, sugar cane, bamboo, brazier cooked foods, curries, rice etc & charcoal
MY SKETCH BOOK IS LIVELY WITH VIVID RAPID DRAWINGS EAGERLY SCRIBBLED

Shallow water fishing - graceful picturesque nets. I saw similar in STOCKHOLM

I never fathomed the facts about this basket fishing, but saw rows of hatted peasants so engaged as we flashed by in a coach.

THESE HATS, ALMOST AS DIFFICULT TO DRAW AS SPIRAL STAIRS & SUN SHADES!

BASKETRY HATS, various styles, with openwork crowns, sit lightly on the head; [& the feet of the seller.]

WATER BUFFALOES clear & harrow paddy fields, pull rice to threshing floor, & thresh it. 2 or 3 harvests according to rains. Birds eat ticks from their muddy backs

PEDAL CYCLISTS 2 OR 3 WHEELERS

SHALL WE COME TO THIS BEFORE N. SEA PETROL COMES ON STREAM? HOW DO THEY BALANCE WITH SUCH LOADS?

Yesterday's River sail, & Temple Visits; today's Floating Markets, concert of Dance, Fencing, Sparring, the parade of elephants, & far east food, all in 2 days! "We could go home now" said M.M.B "We could w/end here for these exotic sights & return home satisfied!"
BUT WE STAYED 17 DAYS.

SUGAR CANES CUT & BOUND FOR SALE. LEAVES OF SUGAR PALM SPROUT FROM STALK TIPS LIKE HUGE DANDELION CLOCKS!

MORE JOLLY SUN HATS & MORE FRIENDLY SAMPANS

A ROW OF THAI HATS ON PEASANTS BENDING OVER THE RICE CROP.

GROWN UPS & CHILDREN WASH & SWIM IN THE KLONGS, [CANALS] DOWN THE STEPS OF THEIR BALCONIED & STILTED ROOMS. GEESE ARE TETHERED, & DUCKS SWIM AROUND ON LEADS.

HUMPING BASKETS OF WHAT I NEVER KNEW.

AROUND CHIENGMAI

1,001' LAT 18

27. 12. 1973

OLD CAPITAL OF SIAM, RICE BOWL OF ASIA, 500 mls N· of Bangkok on mountain fringe "TAKE WOLLIES, IT WILL BE COLD" THEY SAID. IT WAS!

THRESHING

WINNOWING BY SHAKING A TRAY

Driving across the rice plain we saw the bunds which hold water, criss crossing the paddy fields, & peasants hard at work gathering, stooking, stacking, threshing, winnowing the rice.

PEDAL SAMLORS IN THE COUNTRYSIDE & TOWNS

MEO VILLAGE, 3,200'

In a local bus, no glass in the windows; plank wood seats; little head room; we lurched & lolloped up & down twisty hill roads, pitching & tossing, up to this MEO village, where, on s'facing hillside, scorching by day freezing at night, folk spin & weave their clothes, grow their crops [& OPIUM], fashion utensils; wear silver dowries round head, neck & waist, & migrate every few years. I drew like one possessed! at top speed of concentration.

TOPS

BOYS WEAR PANTALOONS

GIRLS WEAR PUTTEES

Babies carried by tiny tots, as well as mums, dads, & grannies.

CRAFTSMANSHIP IN VILLAGES.

"SKILL COMES SO SLOW & LIFE SO FAST DOTH FLY"

"ALL THESE PUT THEIR TRUST IN THEIR HANDS."

We saw cross legged girls, skirts falling modestly, showing just a peep of toe, busily painting lacquer, using gold leaf; weaving baskets; hammering repoussé silver; pulping bark for sunshades; spinning & weaving silk; IN A SERIES OF SPECIALIST VILLAGES WHICH SURROUND CHIENGMAI. MY SKETCH BOOK GLOWS WITH DRAWINGS!

KITES beloved of THAIS [contests in March & April] on sale by roadside. Sellers squatted under banana thatch.

DOI SUTEP TEMPLE

300 steps up, between banister dragon tails, & under scented frangi pani trees, to the Temple terrace, high above a blaze of pointsettias & sunflowers with views for miles. A bewilderment of charm & delight among fantastic temple buildings

SUNG INTRODUCED HIS MUM, A NUN HERE, BARE FEET, SHAVEN HEAD,

TALL, SLENDER SHY & SO VERY PEACEFUL!

LOTUS

sacred to BUDDHA. It rises from mud to beauty [evil to goodness.] Each part is put to use :- stamens flavour tea; rhizomes & young leaves edible; seeds make bread; fruit, wine; stems lamp wicks; & flowers symbolise fertility.

ELEPHANTS

A FINE TUSKER! MAHOUT'S FOOT APPEARS UNDER EAR

ME

PEASANTS TOO, MUFFLED AGAINST COLD!

In teak forests elephants were manipulating logs, cleverly, under clever mahouts. Then down to the river where mahouts performed balancing feats dowsing them while they lurched & wallowed, squirted water & enjoyed being scrubbed; a riveting scene. Again I drew LIKE MAD, SWATHED AGAINST THE COLD, WHILE OTHERS CLICKED THEIR CAMERAS.

PHUKET ISLAND

18·12·73 Fly Sth to _Phuket_, Lat 8°, where we had a bungalow for 2, on stilts & surrounded by coconut palms right on the headland with gd beaches, many off shore islands & astonishing landscapes.

One morning great fronds were pruned & coconuts thinned, so we had fresh coconut milk for breakfast.

20' long fronds fell with a plop & bounce.

A tree grows 80 nuts a year providing food, drink, oil & fat. Every part of the tree is fully used with purpose.

FROM OUR GLASS BOTTOM BOAT WE VIEWED THE MAGICAL BEWITCHING UNDERWATER WORLD OF CORAL GARDENS, TRANSFIXED BY PHOSPHORESCENT FILIGREES AS WE DRIFTED TO AN UNINHABITED OFF SHORE ISLAND, ALL TO OURSELVES. THERE WE 4 BATHED, SWAM, EXPLORED CORAL BEACH & JUNGLE, PADDLED, FOUND SHELLS, & CRABS LIKE THISTLE DOWN, TOOK PICNIC IN FRANGIPANI SHADE.

GLASS BOTTOM LAUNCH

WHAT A CLIMB! MONKEYS WOULD SAY: Q.E.D!

FEET OF NITRA WHO SERVED ICED DRINKS IN CAVES

KEO'S FEET, OUR SKIPPER

But oh! the the RETURN! We 4 elderlies had to bale out the bouncing dingy, cross a choppy sea above sharp corals, then get ourselves up from pitching dingy to rolling launch, & edge our way along its narrow rim to the cabin. NO HELP FROM STEERSMAN! Grazed elbows? Bruised shins? Drenched sketches? sharks? NO! The feat achieved with prowess!

MY THAI HAT

FRUITS

CAVES! Great caverns, ice cold after the heat outside. Grottoes within caves, some up hill some down, a scramble over rocks. STALAGMITES like family groups in sculpture. One cave, a Temple with Buddhas & shrines. OUTSIDE, HIGH ROCK STACKS PUNCTUATE THE LANDSCAPE.

We saw pineapple gdns, fresh ones picked & sliced for our picnic; rubber plantations shady & cool; tin mines, interesting; chillis, peppers, gourds, pomelos, egg-plums, aubergines, mango, papaya, etc fruits of the earth in abundance.

HOUSES RAISED ON HIGH STILTS ABOVE THE SEA

CLEAN STREETS.

WE SAILED BY MANGROVE THICKETS. ARCHED AERIAL ROOTS; CHARCOAL.

SCHOOL BUS

SCHOOL GIRLS EAGER TO TRY THEIR ENGLISH ON US. V.GOOD

OUR LAUNCH

MUMS CHAT

I couldn't believe my eyes looking down from the 'plane on these fangs of rock rising from land & sea, now they were around me. This village, built on a forest of stilts above the mud spit of Koa Panyee Rock is a knock-out sight. These "SEA GYPSIES" look so healthy & alert, children lively, full of fun. They live on fish which they catch & vegetables which they grow. Their streets are tree trunks, their timber houses & school thatched with nipa palm. A happy community I THOUGHT. THIS EXTRAORDINARY SCENE [SEE SKETCH BK DETAILS] SENT ME INTO A TRANCE-LIKE STATE OF ECSTASY & WONDER.

"The leagues of life to greybeards seem
Shorter than boyhood's lingering miles."

Having completed eight decades,
I contemplate the ninth wondering
what further leagues may be in store;
[the appetite grows by what it feeds on]
I hope for a glimpse of China & India
Mexico, Alaska, but will there be time?
Persia, I regret will have to remain
another arm chair conception.

"Cut not my thread,"
said the spider,
"before my web be spun!"

MISERICORD
IN BOSTON P. CHURCH

SQUATTING
BETWIXT
PEWS
SO DARK &
CRAMPED!

GUESS MUCH,
DRAW FAST,
TO AVOID
STIFFNESS!

SCHOOL MASTER BIRCHES BOY
3 OTHERS WAIT THEIR TURN

MISERICORD
IN RIPON CATHEDRAL

GRIFFIN AFTER 2 RABBITS'
LEWIS CARROLL'S BOLTS DOWN HOLE.

This books can do—nor this alone: they give,
New views to life, and teach us how to live;
They soothe the grieved, the stubborn they chastise;
Fools they admonish, and confirm the wise.
Their aid they yield to all: they never shun
The man of sorrow, nor the wretch undone;
Nor tell to various people various things,
But show to subjects what they show to kings.

Here come the grieved, a change of thought to find,
The curious here, to feed a craving mind;
Here the devout their peaceful temple choose;
And here the poet meets his favouring muse.

wrote George Crabbe 1754-1832

◇ ◇ ◇

No diversions then!
◇ ◇ ◇
No Crosswords then
No Television
No Walkman
No Radio!
ONLY BOOKS.

And as for me, thogh that I can but lyte
On bokes for to rede, I me delyte;
And to hem yeve I feyth and ful credence,
And in myn herte have hem in reverence
So hertely, that ther is game noon,
That fro my bokes maketh me to goon,
But hit be seldom, on the holyday;
Save, cerleynly, whan that the month of May
Is comen, and that I here the foules singe
And that the floures ginnen for to springe,
Farwel my boke and my devocion.

Wrote Geoffrey Chaucer 1328-1400.